ADD IN ADULTS

Help for Adults Who Suffer from Attention Deficit Disorder

Dr Gordon Serfontein

SIMON & SCHUSTER
AUSTRALIA

ADD IN ADULTS

First published in Australia in 1994 by
Simon & Schuster Australia
20 Barcoo Street, East Roseville NSW 2069

Reprinted 1994 (twice), 1996

Viacom International
Sydney New York London Toronto Tokyo Singapore

National Library of Australia
Cataloguing in Publication data

Serfontein, Gordon.
  ADD in adults: help for adults who suffer from attention deficit disorder.

  Includes index.
  ISBN 0 7318 0390 6.

  1. Attention-deficit hyperactivity disorder. I. Title.

616.8589

Illustrations by Leslye Cole
Designed by Kathie Baxter Smith/Design Smiths
Typeset in Australia by Asset Typesetting Pty. Ltd.
Printed in Australia by Griffin Paperbacks.

ADD
IN ADULTS

This book is dedicated to my mother and late father, who have supported me throughout my life in all my endeavours.

ACKNOWLEDGMENTS

The Publishers would like to thank Mrs Barbara Serfontein for her assistance with the production of this book, and the staff at the Serfontein Clinic. We would like to express our great appreciation to Dr Geoffrey Kewley (Consultant Paediatrician, Crawley Hospital and the Learning Assessment Centre, Ashdown Hospital, Haywards Heath, West Sussex, UK) for his very helpful interest in the work and for checking details in the text. Our thanks also to Stan Mould (Founder and Chairman of LADDER, the Learning, Hyperactivity and Attention Deficit Disorders Association, England) for his reading of the text and constructive comment. Finally, we would like to thank Dr Christopher Green for writing the foreword and the postscript about Gordon's life.

FOREWORD

Many of Australia's most successful businesspeople, innovators and high-profile personalities have one thing in common — they are adults who still suffer the effects of ADD. Like Einstein and Churchill before them, as children these eminent people felt they were failures at school and incorrectly believed they were unintelligent and inferior. As adults they continue to display poor self-esteem, specific weaknesses in learning, poor short-term memory, a low frustration threshold and social ineptitude. Despite this, they have capitalised on the energy and single-mindedness that goes with ADD and have used it to make their mark.

Gordon Serfontein knew about ADD from a personal perspective. He struggled through school, eventually coming to terms with his strengths and weaknesses. After this he became a 'Top Gun' air force pilot and later pursued his career in medicine with equal pace.

When Gordon started his work many of Australia's most influential leaders in medicine and education did not accept his ideas. The publication of his first book, *The Hidden Handicap*, greatly increased understanding of ADD, and much of the current awareness and improved treatment of the condition has come through his teaching. As Gordon worked in his practice he noted the strong hereditary link in both ADD and Specific Learning Disabilities. Many parents, usually the father, had suffered similarly as a child and a high proportion of these grown-ups had brought their ADD with them to adulthood.

Gordon set his sights on this adult group, writing this second book and preparing to provide some adult-based services in Sydney. Unfortunately he died before he could take this last stage further.

ADD in Adults is a wonderful book in which Gordon covers a complex subject in his clear, simple style. It provides an overview of the subtle difficulties in learning, behaviour and socialisation that arise from ADD. Gordon believed that every child must be given the best possible treatment in their school years so they can enter adulthood with high self-esteem and an ability to use ADD to their advantage.

Though explained simply here, ADD in adults is quite a complex condition. By this stage problems with self-esteem, relationships, frustration, alcoholism and depression can do much to cloud the picture. In such instances, priority needs to be given to the treatment of the specific symptom, rather than to the pursuit of ADD as its possible cause. Gordon's aim with this book was to get us first to recognise the existence of the condition in adults and how it affects their lives. He then suggests ways to help them to redirect their energies from a focus on failure onto the areas that will give them most success. The final suggestion is to seek professional help.

I must emphasise that the ideas in this book are very new, somewhat controversial and, as yet, not universally accepted. I share Gordon's view that ADD will probably become one of the most important new areas of psychology and psychiatry in the next decade. In the meantime, please be patient with the helping professionals. At this moment there are few services geared to the adult with ADD.

Gordon wrote this book to increase awareness. He put the ball in the air, it's now up to those who follow to make the running.

Dr Christopher Green — a friend and colleague.
Consultant Paediatrician, Head of the Child Development Unit, The Children's Hospital, Sydney.
Child-care author.

CONTENTS

INTRODUCTION

My teachers saw me at once backward and precocious, reading books beyond my years and yet at the bottom of the form. They were offended. They had large resources of compulsion at their disposal, but I was stubborn.

Winston Churchill about his schooling.

The publication of my first book, dealing with Attention Deficit Disorder in children, *The Hidden Handicap*, resulted in numerous people from all walks of life contacting me about not only their children but also themselves. These people told me that many of the features I had described still applied to themselves.

I have been written to or visited by doctors, architects, lawyers, judges, builders, insurance-workers, salesmen, housewives, psychologists, teachers, sheet-metal workers, motor mechanics, taxi-drivers, farmers and many others who felt a sense of relief wash over them after reading *The Hidden Handicap*. At last they had discovered the reason for the difficulties they had experienced as children, both at school and at home. They were now quite sure that their problem childhoods were not due to an abnormal personality but could be explained by ADD (Attention Deficit Disorder). For them it was a cathartic experience. I would like to quote here from one such letter:

At age seventeen, I discovered law and was accepted at an institution in Brisbane. I plodded through the year (1977) always dazed at what was required and never quite able to make the connection between persons' conflict and the application of the law. In short, I could not extract the issues. Problems just seemed to be immense and insurmountable. I could not remember sufficient information even to make a suitable application of law. I failed that year. The margins of failure were all about 3 to 5 per cent.

This shook me dramatically. My entrance score to university had been well within what the faculty required and to all intents I should have performed well. I requested and was granted a deferral of one year. My aim was to look for work and try and sort myself out, as well as save some money.

I applied for and was enlisted into the Army in 1978. I am still in the Army and will probably remain with them until the twenty-year mark (1998). I enjoy my job in a limited manner, as it allows me to have other interests and more time for my children. I have been a shift worker for thirteen years. My job involves computers and communications, subjects that interest me but not in a vocational way. However, I am very grateful to my employer that I have been exposed to these concepts as it has probably kept me from leaving the Army. At present, my age is thirty-three years.

A career in law has kept enticing me, however. Your final chapter in the book *The Hidden Handicap* about adults not really knowing what career path they should choose, seemed to fit me well. Five years ago I embarked on tertiary study in valuation, a profession that incorporates substantial law concepts. I lost interest in this after one year, despite doing well in all subjects.

For the last three years I have been tempted to enrol in Law at university but have pulled out my application at the last moment. In 1989 I was actually at the acceptance stage and withdrew. I was frightened beyond belief that it would all happen again and I would be devastated yet again.

I dare to dabble in self-diagnosis and say that my problem is one of concentration and short-term memory. My mind, I believe, is still immature in certain areas.

Recently, I gave a lecture to a large group of parents who were forming an ADD support group in a coastal town near Sydney. It had been raining heavily that day and night, and I had spent about 90 minutes negotiating the occasionally treacherous road from the city to the resort town. Somewhat wet and tired I walked into a lecture room overflowing with parents of children with ADD. After I had given my talk I made myself available for questions which continued for another hour or so. At the end of question time I was packing my lecture notes away and looking forward to returning home and going to bed. When I turned around I was faced by a snaking queue of parents all waiting patiently to talk to me again. They had been too shy to state their questions in front of the large gathering.

I looked at the face of the first person waiting and I could see that he was a man of the outdoors, probably a farmer. He was suntanned, with many of the wrinkles that appear early in those who have spent much of their lives under the sun. He moved toward me and his first words were 'Doc, I want to thank you very much for your talk this evening, as you told me so much about my son. However, you also told me a great deal about myself. Every aspect that you mentioned this evening regarding this condition has affected me for most of my life. Now that I know that something can be done for my son, is there anything that can be done for me?'

This statement and question became the refrain for most of the next hour, as parent after parent spoke to me about their own particular difficulties relating to ADD in childhood and adulthood. Almost without exception they were still experiencing frustrations from the condition and were finding it hard to cope with the various symptoms, mainly because they were unaware of their source and didn't know how to deal with them.

The study and management of ADD in children is, relatively speaking, a new discipline in paediatrics and has been comprehensively studied only for the last three or four decades. The study of adults with this condition is much more rudimentary and is only now starting to receive any consistent attention from researchers.

It has always been known that ADD is one of the most common conditions in children. At first it was thought to be a disorder that gradually improved and eventually resolved itself somewhere in adolescence. There is no doubt that many of the symptoms of ADD improve in middle to late adolescence, and the child who has had some management until then often does quite well. However, it is becoming more apparent that many people (especially those who have not had their condition attended to) continue with various aspects of ADD, albeit with reduced severity, into adulthood. These symptoms affect them in their daily lives and interfere with their academic, family and social interactions.

While driving home that evening after the talk at the coastal town, I reflected upon the fact that I myself had ADD, and had experienced most of the features that so many of the parents there had mentioned to me. I understood their sense of frustration and lack of self-esteem which stem from ADD. On many occasions I have felt similarly vexed when I knew that the ability I had to perform a certain task could not be produced or demonstrated.

In this book I would like to share with all of you who still have difficulties stemming from this condition, the experiences that I have had both as a clinician and also as a person with ADD. I hope that my exploration of its different aspects will help you to recognise the symptoms more readily. Only then can you work towards eliminating or reducing their negative influences, and accentuate and consolidate the positive aspects that ADD can contribute to your career and social encounters.

In the first chapters of this book I summarise the different characteristics of ADD and sketch out the way in which the brain functions in this condition. I then define the particular symptoms and suggest how to counteract their features or turn them to advantage.

As in *The Hidden Handicap*, I have kept the chapters of *ADD in Adults* as brief as possible, mainly because many people with ADD are reluctant, and often poor, readers. I therefore hope that the basic message of the book comes through clearly. I also hope that the book appeals to everyone. I have used plural pronouns throughout, but in some instances the masculine third person pronoun is used and this reflects the male bias of ADD — not any sexism on my part.

CHAPTER ONE

WHAT IS IT ALL ABOUT?

His conduct is exceedingly bad. He is not to be trusted to do any one thing ...
He is a constant trouble to everybody and is always in some scrape or other.

Headmaster of St George's School to Winston Churchill's parents.

The concept of Attention Deficit Disorder (ADD) that has emerged in the past twenty-five years possesses a broader definition than some of the earlier ones for related conditions, such as hyperactivity. It has been increasingly felt that hyperactivity is just one aspect of the wider concept of ADD. Apart from hyperactivity, other core problems of the disorder include poor concentration, impulsiveness, easy distractability, as well as problems with speech, co-ordination, short-term memory and associated behavioural and learning difficulties. However, until recently, the symptom of hyperactivity has been regarded as the main problem in ADD, and clinical management and research have concentrated on this aspect.

The hyperactive child and adult have probably been around since the emergence of modern man. Hyperactive characters abound in literature: the main characters in cartoons such as *Dennis the Menace* and *The Katzenjammer Kids*; German literature contains children such as Max and Moritz and Struwel Peter; and fictional characters such as Tom Jones, created by Henry Fielding, display all the features of hyperactivity.

STUDY

Despite the description of ADD in well-researched papers, many doctors still doubted the existence of the condition, and it was frequently referred to as the 'diagnosis without a disease'.

In the 1950s studies indicated that one-third of hyperactive children studied showed non-specific abnormalities in their electroencephalograms. In the early 1970s Dr Paul Wender of Salt Lake City suggested that the condition had a neuro-chemical basis. Research carried out during the 1970s and 1980s did indeed establish a neurochemical basis for the disorder. The neurochemistry of ADD is discussed in detail in Chapter 3, A System of Balances.

TERMINOLOGY

Earlier this century it was considered that children with Hyperkinetic-impulse Disorder and Minimal Brain Dysfunction had two separate and distinct disorders. The former was characterised by overactivity, impulsiveness, poor concentration and a low frustration threshold. The latter, by specific learning disabilities, in association with developmental dysfunctions such as speech aberrations, lack of co-ordination and minor indications of neurological problems; it also, at times, incorporated some of the features of Hyperkinetic-impulse Disorder.

A number of researchers in the last twenty years have given increasing importance to the symptoms of Hyperkinetic Impulse Disorder. Thus the features of this disorder came to be considered as part of the one disorder, incorporating the symptoms of both Hyperkinetic Impulse Disorder and Minimal

Brain Dysfunction. The need arose for a more general term to reflect this new understanding.

The American Psychiatric Association, in its *Diagnostic and Statistics Manual of Mental Disorders (DSM-III)*, collated all the relevant criteria for this condition and called it 'Attention Deficit Disorder'. It also defined two sub-categories of the condition: ADD with or without hyperactivity. The characteristics of children with ADD and hyperactivity correlated with those identified in Hyperkinetic-impulse Disorder; the diagnosis for children with ADD only, was similar to that for Minimal Brain Dysfunction.

WHAT IS ADD?

Attention Deficit Disorder is a developmental dysfunction of the central nervous system, which occurs more frequently in males. It is a genetic condition whose behavioural features may become more evident in the first year of life, but more often appear by the age of seven. It seems that the central nervous system of affected children does not develop at a rate consistent with that of their peers. Depending on how much of the system is involved, and the severity of the developmental lag, the child displays one or more of the symptoms of ADD.

The disorder appears to reach its peak between the ages of eight and fifteen, followed in many cases by a spontaneous improvement. It seems that the immature sections of the brain are involved in some 'catch-up' in later adolescence. However, a significant proportion of people continue with some symptoms into adulthood — the so-called Attention Deficit Disorder Residual type (ADD-R).

SYMPTOMS OF ADD

The major symptoms of ADD may be conveniently divided into two categories: academic and behavioural. Just how these symptoms manifest themselves in adulthood is explained in subsequent chapters. However, to give you an overall picture of the difficulties people with ADD face, following is a brief list of the symptoms and how they affect children.

Academic difficulties

Brief attention span
Affected children find it hard to focus and sustain attention, and tend to daydream or be destructive. They frequently procrastinate and find it difficult to amuse themselves.

Short-term memory deficiencies
Difficulty in retaining newly acquired information long enough for reinforcement (which normally occurs on re-exposure, and results in consigning the information to long-term memory) seems to be a prominent feature of this condition. It leads to learning difficulties, poor response to instructions, and an inability to learn symbols such as colours and the alphabet.

Speech disorders
Many of these children are slow to develop verbal expression and sentence construction (frequently beyond three years of age), have sequencing problems (melonade for lemonade), stutter, and have various other difficulties including mumbling.

Co-ordination

Many children with ADD have developmental problems which affect their gross- or fine- motor skills, or their eye/hand co-ordination. They have difficulties with balance, hopping, running, riding a bicycle (gross-motor skills); with handwriting and doing up buttons and laces (fine-motor skills); or with catching balls, throwing, and kicking (eye/hand/foot co-ordination).

Perception

These children often have problems with correctly identifying, discriminating, sequencing, blending or analysing shapes or sounds. These difficulties are very likely to lead to specific learning disabilities. Some children even have problems integrating visual and auditory stimuli, a process vital for composite learning.

Organisational skills

Organisational skills are often weak. Children may show lower than ordinary ability to organise their rooms, daily activities or schoolwork. This problem is often apparent in examinations: children with the disorder cannot discern which answers have top priority and therefore obtain lower marks than those they obtain for class assessments.

Behavioural abnormalities

Overactivity

Children with ADD have great difficulty sitting still for long stretches of time. Depending on the severity of the condition, their behaviour will range from fidgetiness to restlessness, and even to moving around physically or being decidedly hyperactive. A few children are of the classically hyperactive type that can destroy the home in five minutes.

Impulsiveness

Children with this symptom give very little thought to the consequences of their actions. 'Act before you think' is their motto and so they run across roads without looking, climb up high roofs, jump from dangerous heights, light fires, play with explosives, and so on. They put their own safety at great risk and frequently risk that of others. This impulsiveness can also be verbal, and many of these children seem to think aloud all the time.

Low frustration threshold

From early childhood, children with ADD find it difficult to cope with being frustrated or thwarted in their desires. Their response is either to have a temper outburst and become aggressive, or withdraw from the frustration without trying to deal with it. It is a major cause of household disruption and family fractures.

Low self-esteem

Self-esteem is almost always low in children with this condition. Low self-esteem seems to have primary and secondary elements. Many very young children with ADD are reluctant to play with their peers and prefer younger children, which suggests a primary deficiency of their self-image. When they do not progress at school or do not develop social skills, a secondary exacerbation of the negative self-image usually ensues.

Inflexibility

These children frequently have problems in adjusting to anything new: schools, teachers, kids on the block, homes, clothes — you name it, if it's new they will most probably have problems with it. They seem to prefer a very steady routine and a consistent, familiar environment where they know what to expect. This inflexibility often leads to a higher level of frustration. Not all children with ADD display all symptoms, but those they do exhibit often continue into adulthood.

As mentioned, expression of these symptoms in adults is what we are concerned with in this book, and is discussed in Chapters 4 to 12.

KEY POINTS
- The study of Attention Deficit Disorder (ADD) over the past twenty-five years is the result of earlier research into hyperactivity, which until recently was considered the main problem.
- Other symptoms of the disorder include: concentration and short-term memory problems; speech disorders; poor co-ordination; problems with perception; organisational difficulties; impulsiveness; low frustration threshold; poor self-esteem; and inflexibility.
- ADD is a developmental disorder of the central nervous system.
- It is a genetic condition which affects mostly males, and its features become apparent in childhood.
- Depending on the severity of the developmental lag, children affected by ADD display one or more of its symptoms.

CHAPTER TWO

COMMON AS A COLD

They will say & with some reason that you can't stick to anything ... I confess I am quite disheartened about you. You seem to have no real purpose in life & won't realise at the age of twenty-two that for a man life means work, & hard work if you mean to succeed.

Lady Randolph Churchill to her son, Winston.

If you have ADD rest assured that you are not alone. Research over the last decade has shown that between 30 and 70 per cent of all children with the disorder continue to exhibit symptoms as adults. Based on a conservative estimate that 5 per cent of children have ADD, somewhere between 2 and 4 per cent of all adults have significant difficulties as a result of the condition. Therefore, if you do not have ADD, you probably know someone who does.

Evidence of ADD continuing into adulthood is found in adults who, as children, were treated with drug therapy for this condition and who continue to benefit noticeably from treatment. It is because ADD so commonly persists into adulthood that the adult form is called 'Attention Deficit Disorder, Residual State'. This implies that ADD is not always resolved in adolescence as previously thought, and that it can maintain its pervasive influence into adult life.

The incidence of ADD in children appears to be much greater in boys than girls, by a ratio of about 10:1. However, in adults the ratio changes somewhat to vary between 1:1 and 6:1. This may indicate that women who had a mild form of the condition as children experience more difficulties in adulthood because of its longstanding effects upon their concentration, organisational skills, and so on.

The incidence of this condition varies from country to country, according to the criteria used for diagnosis. In the United States the rate ranges from 5 per cent to as high as 22 per cent. In Australia, a study by the University of Queensland found that the incidence among Australian males is 18 per cent. When boys and girls are taken together, the rate of incidence ranges from 8 to 12 per cent. Even at its lowest rate of incidence, ADD appears to be a major childhood disorder.

Other research shows that when ADD persists into adulthood it does not remain a pure disorder possessing only those features outlined in Chapter 1. In one study only 14 per cent of afflicted adults had ADD as their main dysfunction. The rest had experienced significant problems with their self-esteem, learning and interaction with society, which had led to secondary associated conditions. The most prominent among these included anxiety, drug and/or alcohol abuse, depression and mood swings. These problems were directly due to the persistence of the condition.

However, there is clear evidence that many adults with ADD function at a higher occupational level than the general population. Therefore, if you have been diagnosed with ADD, remember that it does not always lead to a poor outcome. Many people afflicted with ADD are able to develop natural strategies either to overcome the worst features of the condition or to convert some of its positive features into more productive attributes. If you have not yet learned how to do this, Chapters 4 to 12 in particular will help you.

Although adults with ADD who were not treated as

children appear to have no different symptoms from those who were, treatment in childhood does greatly reduce the likelihood of secondary problems occurring later in life. It lowers the incidence of secondary depression of dysphoria (diminished feeling of well-being) and improves the self-esteem and learning ability of adults. If you take into account that between 50 and 80 per cent of children with ADD develop significant learning problems, it is logical to assume that this will affect their later lives considerably if they do not receive early intervention.

It is possible that the incidence of ADD in adults is greater than between the 2 and 4 per cent suggested at the opening of this chapter. At least one study shows that many adults with ADD have been mistakenly diagnosed as having one of the psychoses (abnormal thought processes), such as schizophrenia. One of the major features of schizophrenia is a tendency to take words at their literal meaning — the person can seldom perceive figurative (non-literal) meaning. This literal-mindedness is also a common feature of ADD, and this is how the two conditions may be confused.

There seems to be little doubt that ADD runs in families, but it has no specific pattern of inheritance. It is common for people with ADD to have at least one other member of their immediate family also display strong features of the condition.

Research shows that boys adopted at an early age and brought up in settled homes nevertheless developed hyperactivity if their biological fathers were hyperactive. Also adopted children with ADD whose natural fathers are alcoholics experience a higher rate of later alcohol abuse than adopted children who do not have ADD. In the case of twins, studies show that if one of a pair of identical twins has ADD, there is a 100 per cent incidence in the other twin. In non-identical twins, the incidence rate drops to the national level of between 15 and 19 per cent.

You will see from all the evidence so far that ADD not only exists in adults but is also almost as prevalent as the common cold. As we treat the common cold with a variety of support mechanisms and therapies, so too should we approach the problem of ADD — if we do this comprehensively, we will reach a successful outcome.

KEY POINTS

- Approximately 30 to 70 per cent of all children with ADD continue to exhibit symptoms of the disorder as adults. The condition does not always resolve in childhood as previously thought.
- The adult form of ADD is known as ADD-R (Attention Deficit Disorder, Residual State).
- Its incidence is much higher in boys than in girls, however in adults the gap decreases.
- ADD which persists into adulthood often leads to secondary associated problems such as anxiety, depression, and drug and alcohol abuse. Treatment of the condition in childhood decreases the risk of secondary problems occurring later in life.
- In spite of the problems associated with the disorder, ADD sufferers can and do develop strategies to overcome the worst features of their condition and lead very successful lives.
- ADD is a hereditary disorder.

CHAPTER THREE

A SYSTEM OF BALANCES

The human body has natural check mechanisms that operate between various processes to ensure that no single process exists at the cost of another. For instance, if you are given a great big scare, your body releases hormones called adrenalins to help you to deal with the cause of your fright. These circulate throughout the body and bring the muscles into readiness, even to the extent of withdrawing vital nutrients from other organs so that the muscles are well primed for action. This is what allows us to move very quickly, and sometimes with above-human speed, either to run away from or attack a threatening force. This reaction is known as the flight or fight response.

However, if this response continued, your accelerated metabolism would deplete your resources and you would become flaccid, weak and lack motivation. So to avoid this depressed state, the adrenalin release is subsequently counteracted. This also prevents damage to any other organs that had to sacrifice their nutrients for the sake of the muscle groups. Therefore, a balance is required between the initial stimulation and subsequent inactivation of the adrenalin group to keep the body's systems intact.

The medical term for this balancing process is *homeostasis*, a Greek word which basically means 'keeping the state of the body at a constant level'. In the brain it exists at both macroscopic and microscopic levels.

THE MACROSCOPIC LEVEL

The brain is the most complex of our organs and appears to be developing all the time. It also has two basic areas, one of stimulus and one of inhibition. The older part of the brain, which is situated in the middle and is called the diencephalon (or limbic system), is the section responsible for stimulating the rest of the brain. Information fed to the central nervous system through our senses is processed and analysed at this halfway station; stimulatory messages are then sent up to the higher centres of the brain which are situated in the neocortex. The neocortex then inhibits the stimuli coming up from the diencephalon and in this way achieves a state of balance between the two sections (see Figure 1, page 14).

The diencephalon comprises many of the structures that are of primary importance in lower-order animals. It is responsible for vigilance over changes in the environment, as well as the ability to discriminate what is important for a certain function and to focus exclusively upon that particular stimulus at the exclusion of all else. This is how an animal can select what is important for procreation or survival. The diencephalon initiates the animal's moods and motivations, and the animal reacts by, for example, mating, or moving towards food or away from danger.

The short-term retention of information is another function of the diencephalon. An animal's ability to recall immediate changes in its environment is vital to its making an appropriate decision about how to react. The diencephalon is also responsible for the rapid, almost impulsive responses that an animal needs, along with rapid reflexes, for quick movement. In addition, it co-ordinates muscle movements to make them smoother and more efficient.

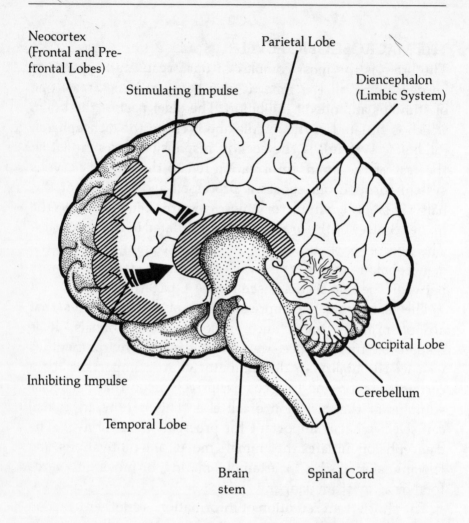

Neocortex
(Frontal and Pre-
frontal Lobes)

Stimulating Impulse

Parietal Lobe

Diencephalon
(Limbic System)

Inhibiting Impulse

Temporal Lobe

Brain
stem

Spinal Cord

Cerebellum

Occipital Lobe

Figure 1 This diagram illustrates the position of main sections of the brain — in particular those affected by ADD, including the diencephalon and the neocortex. The arrows on the diagram indicate a stimulus travelling from the diencephalon to the neocortex and the corresponding inhibitory impulse which the neocortex issues to counteract the increased activity in the brain provided by the stimulus. In this way balance is maintained in the functioning of the brain.

In the human brain, a newer area has developed which exists largely at the front of the brain and is referred to as the neocortex (or prefrontal lobes). This appears to be an area of inhibition that moderates the impulses sent up from the diencephalon, in this way preventing the animal's reactions from being too precipitate or excessive for the required task. In other words, it is a modulating centre where the lower order of diencephalon processes are smoothed, altered and made somewhat more sophisticated as a result of inhibition by this higher centre of the brain.

Our understanding of the new part of the brain is still very limited. However, we do know that it is involved with functions relating to aggression and the organisation of the environment. It also has something to do with the ability to control frustrations and impulsive responses, and the ability to stabilise mood swings that result from the constant stimulation of the diencephalon. The neocortex has other functions related to memory (especially long-term memory), language and communication, and conceptual thinking. These functions are discussed in subsequent chapters.

In the developing brain of the young child and adolescent, balance (homeostasis) is constantly sought between these two systems so that one does not dominate the other. However, based on its prior origin, we assume that the diencephalon develops at an even earlier stage and has a more forceful effect on the very young child. The neocortex, the new part of the brain, develops at a slower rate; only in middle to late adolescence does it reach its full expression and maturity and successfully matches the diencephalon. For this reason, young children are often impulsive and aggressive and find it difficult to contain their immediate desires or thoughts. As they mature they become able to make more thoughtful decisions and gain better control over their immediate desires. By the time children have grown up they have reached the state of equilibrium between the neocortex and the diencephalon.

In the adult with ADD, it seems that this balance is upset or has not developed appropriately, either because the diencephalon is overactive or because the neocortex and its inhibition of the diencephalon have not matured properly. In some cases, both malfunctions occur.

In children with ADD this imbalance between the two forces is greater than in their peers, and results in failure to develop the check mechanisms necessary for both learning and behaviour. These children maintain a certain impulsiveness, and tend to be overactive. They find it difficult to distinguish and focus upon a particular stimulus in the environment well enough to carry out a task successfully. They have quite a large variation in their moods and show the aggression and lack of impulse control common in these children. From a cognitive point of view, their abilities to retain new information or to process it appropriately may also be below par. The end result is people who do not appear to have gained the advantages of age and maturity and still display the behavioural features of young children.

THE MICROSCOPIC LEVEL

Homeostasis exists at a cellular or microscopic level as well.

When your eyes receive the image of a flower, for example, that image creates an electrical charge at the optic nerve where it is registered. The image is then transmitted to the occipital lobe (the visual processing area) at the back of the brain. Here it is interpreted and compared with what you have experienced before. If the occipital lobe considers the image to be new then it is categorised and stored.

The transmission of the image between the eye and the occipital lobe occurs by brain cells, or neurons, linking up to each other to transmit the information between those two particular regions — very much like the passing of a football between players. As in football, where there is a gap between each player which the ball must cross, so too in the nervous system is there a gap between the cells which the impulse must traverse. The impulse crosses this gap with the assistance of chemical fluids called neurotransmitters.

Figure 2 (page 18) shows an incoming message (such as the image of the flower) prompting the release of neurotransmitter fluid into the space between two brain cells. This transmitter fluid carries the impulse to the next cell where it attaches itself to the outer membrane of that cell, so that the second cell becomes stimulated and the message is passed on. Once the neurotransmitter fluids have completed their task, they are broken down and excreted through the body's urine.

Further natural check mechanisms are in place to ensure that the neurotransmitters do not overstay their welcome and cause the second cell to remain in a state of constant stimulation. This would make it unresponsive to new stimuli. As mentioned in the caption for Figure 2, these check mechanisms include enzymes which destroy the extraneous neurotransmitters, as well as the ability of the preceding cell also to reabsorb them. There are a few other such check mechanisms but the basic result is, once again, a balance between stimulus and inhibition.

In people with ADD, the various balancing mechanisms

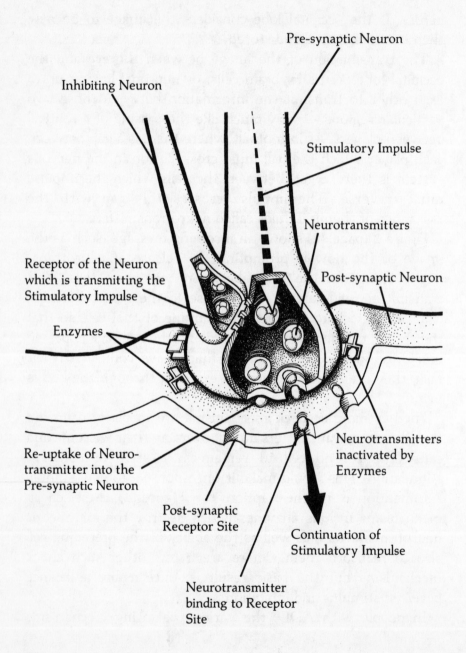

Pre-synaptic Neuron

Inhibiting Neuron

Stimulatory Impulse

Neurotransmitters

Receptor of the Neuron
which is transmitting the
Stimulatory Impulse

Post-synaptic Neuron

Enzymes

Re-uptake of Neuro-
transmitter into the
Pre-synaptic Neuron

Neurotransmitters
inactivated by
Enzymes

Post-synaptic
Receptor Site

Continuation of
Stimulatory Impulse

Neurotransmitter
binding to Receptor
Site

involved in this neural transmission do not function properly. There may be insufficient production of the neurotransmitters, or the enzymes may be too efficient in destroying them; the re-uptake process may be exaggerated or the receptor sites may not bind as well as they should with the neurotransmitters. The end result is that a breakdown in neural transmission occurs, either at the diencephalon or at the neocortex, and causes the clinical features of ADD.

Figure 2 *This figure illustrates the chemical processes involved in ensuring that a stimulus is appropriately recorded and responded to.*

The stimulating electrical impulse travels from the diencephalon via a neuron (brain cell) to the synaptic cleft, the connection point of the brain cells through which the impulse needs to pass. The impulse causes the release of neurotransmitters (dopamine and noradrenaline) which carry it across the synaptic cleft. The neurotransmitters attach themselves to the receptors on the membrane of the second neuron which then receives the impulse. Of the neurotransmitters released, there only needs to be enough of them to stimulate the receiving neuron. The extraneous neurotransmitters are inactivated by enzymes, undergo reabsorption into the pre-synaptic cell (the neuron that discharged the impulse) or fail to bind to the receptors on the post-synaptic cell (the neuron that receives the impulse). These are all normal physiological measures to ensure that the balance is not disturbed.

Also demonstrated is an inhibiting neuron from the neocortex. Neural transmission in this case is similar to that of the excitatory neuron, except that inhibitory neurotransmitters (such as gamma amino butyric acid, GABA) are released by the electrical charge. This inhibition exerted by the neocortex contributes to a balance between the neocortex and the diencephalon, and results in the appropriate response to stimuli.

KEY POINTS

- Our bodies have certain processes (such as the flight or fight response) which keep their various mechanisms in a state of balance.
- The brain also possesses such balancing systems. It has two basic areas of stimulus and inhibition. The **diencephalon** (limbic system) is responsible for stimulating the rest of the brain; it receives messages from the senses and passes them on to other areas. The higher centre of the brain, present only in humans, is the **neocortex** (frontal and prefrontal lobes) which moderates the impulses sent up from the diencephalon.
- In the person with ADD, the balance between the diencephalon and the neocortex is upset or does not develop properly. This results in failure to develop the necessary check mechanisms to learning and behaviour.
- The neocortex is also responsible for the functions involved in aggression and organisation, impulsiveness, mood swings, memory, language, communication and conceptual thinking.
- The necessary balance for the proper functioning of the brain is apparent at a microscopic level. The brain cells connecting the two areas of the brain affected by ADD are unable to function properly. The neurotransmitters which carry impulses from one cell to the next (via the synapses) may not be properly deactivated by enzymes or fail to be reabsorbed into the first cell (resulting in over-stimulation), or may fail to connect with the succeeding cell (resulting in the message not being passed on).

CHAPTER FOUR

CONCENTRATION AND MEMORY

I think the boy means well but he is distinctly inclined to be inattentive...

Tutor of Winston Churchill to Lord Randolph Churchill,
Winston's father.

The function (and dysfunction) that lends its name to ADD is *attention*. As discussed in Chapter 3, attention is crucial to the survival of any organism. It consists of at least four different aspects:

• First, you have to be *conscious* of your environment, so that you can take in information.

• Secondly, you need to be *continously aware* of changes occurring in that environment.

• Thirdly, you should be able to *distinguish* which stimuli are most important for a certain function. For instance, while a spectator is watching a tennis match, he should be able to tell that the action of putting the ball over the net is not a continuous one and is interrupted by frequent breaks. Discerning the variation in the rhythm of the play allows him to relax his concentration whenever the action ceases.

• The fourth and final element of attention is that of *concentration*. You must be able to focus on one (or at the most two) stimuli from the environment and hold it at the exclusion of all else for as long as it takes to register and process it.

Once you have selected and focused upon an important stimulus, it is then necessary for you to hold that stimulus long enough in your memory so that it can be perceived. This function of short-term memory is crucial to the acquisition of information as well as the execution of any task. If it is important enough it should be held until a second reinforcement of that stimulus can enhance its value to the central nervous system so that it is consigned to long-term memory. If information is not retained in the brain until it has been reinforced, it will be either lost or processed in a truncated form, often erroneously.

Note: The faculties of attention and short-term memory are inextricably linked. Whilst short-term memory is sometimes regarded as the final step in the spectrum of attention, it appears to be a part of the central nervous system that is anatomically distinct from the part responsible for attention and may be considered as a separate entity.

ATTENTION AND ADD

People with ADD have difficulties with the last three steps of attention as well as with short-term memory (assuming that they are conscious of their environment). They encounter problems in being vigilant and often miss vital clues that are essential for a cetain performance. They frequently find difficulties in discriminating between stimuli, and in the tennis match described above give as much importance and time to what the drink-seller in the stand may do as to the action taking place on the court. People with a concentration problem find it difficult to bring all their energies to bear upon one stimulus and to exclude the others. For them the problem is not one of distraction, but is one of focusing their thoughts for a period of time. They may have no impairment of the earlier steps — just difficulty with concentration.

When people with a short-term memory problem acquire information, they sometimes cannot hold it long enough for processing and reinforcement, and so when that same information is presented again it is almost as if it is something completely new. Or else they might recall that they have learnt it before, but find they can recollect only fragments, which causes them enormous frustration at their inability to exercise their memory appropriately.

Most people have problems with retaining information that is listened to or read, reading being a verbal task. A minority have difficulties in attending to and retaining visual information. A few people have problems with both visual and verbal attention and memory, and have profound problems with reading and spelling which can often only be assisted by drug therapy.

IMPROVING YOUR ATTENTION

How does one compensate for these deficits? The first step is to establish what your strength is: visual memory or auditory memory. If your ability to retain visual stimuli is much better, then any information you acquire through verbal means needs to be reinforced or supported by a visual aid. For example, if you are attending a lecture that is essentially verbal, you need to make your own visual supplements for it. A notepad in which aspects of the speech can be visualised and abbreviated is an important means of using your visual strength. Conversely, if the lecture content is mainly visual and you have problems with visual attention and memory, you could make a tape-recording which may be played back later, or again make abbreviated written notes to supplement the visual features. Both processes — visualising and verbalising — support the weak mode while exercising the strength of the other mode.

You can employ other strategies to focus your attention, such as sitting in the front row so that the only stimuli that reach you are coming from the speaker. The further back you sit the more stimuli there are to impinge upon your senses.

If you have problems with your auditory attention and memory, and are being introduced to someone, you will frequently experience the embarrassing situation where you have been told the person's name and forget it just a couple of minutes later. In situations such as these you should use the strategy of taking in some visual aspect of the person (for instance, a brooch or tie) and blowing that up ten times its size in your mind; link the person's name with this image by imagining it in a very large written form. By associating some visual image of the person with their name in this way, you will be able to fix it in your mind, and if it is reinforced within a couple of minutes, it will be consigned to your long-term memory.

Similarly, some people can remember names but not faces. They can use a similar strategy: visualising the face and repeating the name softly, almost at the level that one uses in silent thought or prayer, to reinforce the verbal component with the visual image. The essential aids to short-term memory are the frequent and repetitive reinforcement of the initial stimuli to allow its retention in long-term memory.

It is often necessary to maintain vigilance in order to remain focused upon the information being presented. We are all familiar with situations where, during a long and tedious lecture, we start to drift off and think about other things.

That is a natural thing to do, but in people with ADD it happens more frequently and more quickly. You should therefore employ some sort of strategy to enhance your vigilance of the environment and the speaker, and to help you concentrate on the subject at hand. For example, try simple aids such as setting an alarm on your watch to go off at some interval to bring you back to attention; or putting some stickers on your file or folder with time-slots written on them to be removed at appropriate intervals as visual reminders to keep you focused.

Young apprentices often have difficulties concentrating on verbal instructions, although they have no problems in paying visual attention to the work. Here again, a strategy of 'chunking' — breaking up the information into its components — will help an apprentice to relate each instruction to a specific visual task. This is an invaluable strategy for people with ADD and allows them not only to focus upon the information being acquired, but also to give it some logical structure.

With an awareness of the difficulties involved in ADD and by incorporating certain strategies to overcome these, you should not only be able to make up for the handicap imposed by the condition, but employ those strategies in your daily life, thereby improving both your social and working environments.

KEY POINTS

- The four aspects of attention include: consciousness; awareness of the environment; an ability to distinguish appropriate stimuli; and concentration.
- Concentration is necessary for short-term memory: a feature crucial to the aquisition of information, long-term memory and the execution of any task.
- People with ADD encounter problems with concentration and short-term memory, and sometimes with discrimination.
- The disorder tends to affect auditory attention and memory, rather than visual.
- Strategies to help you overcome these problems include: making notes and highlighting important details; and tape-recording lectures (if your auditory memory is stronger).

CHAPTER FIVE

SPEECH AND LANGUAGE

Englishman 25 years old ... average build, walks with a slight stoop, pale appearance ... speaks through the nose, cannot pronounce the letter "s" ...

Capture notice put out by Boers following Winston Churchill's escape from Pretoria.

Difficulty with speech and language is a pervasive feature of ADD. It has been estimated that up to 60 per cent of people with the disorder have problems with the development of their language, whether written, spoken or read.

In young children, the problem presents itself frequently with a delay in the onset of speech. Usually their verbal expression is delayed until the age of four or even five. When talking is established, these children have difficulties with forming and articulating the various sounds. These involve most of the consonants, but especially the words that begin with s, l, r, th, f and v. Such early articulation problems may resolve in childhood without any help, or continue and become established features of the person's speech. We are all well acquainted with lisping, which is a prominent expression of this impairment, and know of several prominent people who have achieved success despite (sometimes because of) their lisp. Whereas a lisp can be a charming attribute, the same cannot always be said of someone who has difficulties in pronouncing 'r'. A child or adult who has difficulty pronouncing 'r' is often teased or even held up to ridicule.

Other early problems in speech include delays in sequencing

sounds, a feature that sometimes continues into adulthood. I have heard several adults with ADD, especially when they are tired, display these problems — they result in spoonerisms, for instance, 'the grey day' comes out as 'the dray gay'. Many of us do this when we are tired, but it is much more persistent in people with ADD. This sequential difficulty not only affects the sounds within words but also the syntax of sentences. A father may want to say to his son: 'Johnny, jump up and get me that book', but says instead: 'Johnny, up jump and get me that book'.

Hesitation or straight-out stuttering are also common and reflect a combination of self-esteem and self-confidence problems and diminished short-term memory. Children find it difficult to hold mentally the various sounds of a word, as well as the words within a sentence, long enough to allow the completion of an idea and then verbalise it. By the time they say a word they have lost some of the elements of what they had intended to say, and this makes them pause to recollect the word structures before attempting once more. If this continues into adulthood, it becomes a habit that is hard to correct. The problem becomes more pronounced when compounded by stress, as we all have difficulties in recalling information when we are anxious.

The inability to project their personality through speech is another problem for people with ADD. Because of the self-esteem problems that come with this condition, these people tend not to speak up clearly, usually in the hope that they will not be heard. It is almost as if they are ashamed of what they have to say and do not want to be taken to task by the listener. As a result, they speak indistinctly; this is not an articulation problem but largely a matter of low sound level.

This habit of speaking under their breath becomes more prominent as these people get older and become less confident of their performance in the public arena.

Where impulsiveness is part of the condition, people with ADD speak very quickly, almost desperately, as if everything they have to say has to be said in one minute. They often speak so rapidly that their words run into each other and become indistinct; also, some words or even groups of words are excluded from a sentence. The brain in each of these people is moving ahead at such a pace that their vocal expression cannot keep up. As a result these people have great difficulty in slowing down and matching their vocal delivery appropriately to their thought process. Their thoughts are usually miles ahead of what is actually being said at the time and a lot of information is lost because of the truncated speech pattern.

There are situations where as much as possible needs to be said in a short space of time. Auctioneers have to impart information quickly so that time is not wasted and the auction can move onto the next lot. Often politicians have to speak at a galloping pace, so that the audience does not have time to digest properly what is being said and they can thus avoid sticky questions at the end of the session. But for people with ADD the speed is not intentional, and it affects both their public and private lives.

It is probably in the area of written language that the greatest impediments occur. In speech we can often disguise verbal deficiencies or divert attention from them, for example with hand movements and facial expressions. However, in written language this is more difficult. People with ADD have great difficulty in transferring their thought processes onto paper. It seems that written expression requires a larger store of short-term memory and greater interplay between different cognitive skills than spoken language does. (Cognitive skills are intellectual or learning skills. Different parts of the brain have different intellectual functions and the interplay occurs between these areas.) As a result, people with ADD develop written expressive styles that are easily diagnosed as part of their condition. Their written work is usually quite abbreviated, even telegrammatic. They have difficulty with completing ideas within a sentence, arranging the syntax correctly, and organising paragraphs. They are weak in formulating an idea, developing it and recapitulating.

These people experience great frustration with essay-style subjects at school, and performances are better in scientific subjects where short one-point answers are required. In many cases their impulsiveness and over-rapid thought processes further handicap their written expression by causing them to delete words or sentences. Teachers are quite well acquainted with the essays that these people produce — all they want to say is said in one paragraph at the top of the page. However, they have difficulties in developing these ideas, interrelating them, and enriching the initial thought. If the person with ADD has none of the speech problems outlined so far, when asked to express ideas verbally, they are often able to embellish and develop them with amazing depth and intricacy — in contrast to their written expression. Asking a person with ADD to give a verbal account of his opinion is often like granting a convicted prisoner a reprieve. They visibly relax and everything they have to say comes out in a much more understandable format.

You can see from all this that difficulties with speech, language, and written expression would cause significant problems in adulthood. One of the major attributes of human beings is that they can communicate with their species through language, both spoken and written. If a person's ability to communicate is diminished by a condition such as ADD, it seriously restricts his capacity to present, not only himself and his personality, but also his knowledge and ideas in a way that would be acceptable and show him at his best.

Written applications for new positions seldom reflect these people's capabilities because their underdeveloped written expression gives the impression that they are poorly educated. As jobs are becoming scarcer today, employers usually cull applicants by means of their written application. People with ADD are always liable to lose out in the first round of selection due to their poor written presentation. Those who do make it through the first round then have to present themselves for an interview. Difficulties with their speech, articulation or verbal language formulation will hinder them in the interview and prevent them from demonstrating their true abilities.

IMPROVING YOUR SPEECH AND LANGUAGE SKILLS

It is important that adults with ADD who have not had any help with their speech, language or written expression should consult a professional over these matters. Your first port of call should be a good speech pathologist or elocutionist. An elocutionist will not only improve the basic nuts and bolts of speech, such as articulation, and remove hesitancy and stuttering, but will also help improve your self-esteem and self-confidence so that your voice projection matches your true personality. Elocution also helps you to present an idea coherently in the shortest space possible.

Another worthwhile port of call is a good remedial teacher for coaching in written expression. You may not necessarily want to be a Charles Dickens, but you may feel that there is a distinct need to improve not only the style, but also the content of your written work. It is my experience that a short course of coaching in essay-writing skills produces blue-chip results in the long term.

The investment of some time and money in these areas will bring lifelong rewards, not only in the academic arena but also in social situations. Confidence in addressing people at school functions or social clubs or even writing personal letters will benefit, as a flow-on, your general demeanour and attitude, and in this way enrich your life in general.

KEY POINTS

- Speech and language (including writing and reading) difficulties are pervasive features of ADD.
- Speech problems include the late onset of talking; lisping, dyslexia, stuttering, not speaking clearly, speaking too quickly.
- Writing problems include an abbreviated expressive style, an inability to complete ideas within a sentence, and problems with arranging syntax, organising paragraphs and developing an idea logically.
- Those with writing problems experience great difficulty with essay-style subjects at school, and often prefer more scientific ones that require one-point answers. In regard to developing their ideas, they are often much better at this if asked to do so verbally.
- The inability to communicate effectively can cause significant problems in adulthood, for example, writing out a résumé or job application becomes an even more tortuous task.
- Strategies that help you to overcome these problems include: seeking professional help (for example, from a speech pathologist); and tutoring in written expression.

CHAPTER SIX

READING AND WRITING

Writing —good but so terribly slow. Spelling — is about as bad as it well can be.

The seven-year-old Winston Churchill's report
from St George's School.

Many, if not most, people with ADD are reluctant readers and writers. For them the exercise of reading and writing is a tiring, tedious and often unrewarding exercise. It is laborious for them to decode words, analyse them, reconstitute them and express them in written form. Throughout school, and also in their adult lives, they are people who do not read for pleasure, and certainly do not write for pleasure. They are poor letter-writers and fail to keep correspondence for this reason. They would rather use the telephone or engage in direct speech (even if they have speech problems) than develop any skill at letter-writing. Reading is done purely for factual information necessary for career development. Reading novels or other lengthy literature is not pursued as a recreational pastime. Let us look at some of the reasons why people with ADD resist reading and writing. To fully understand the processes of these activities I will run through the cognitive steps involved in these functions.

PROCESSES INVOLVED IN READING AND WRITING
When a person is attending to a word (for example, 'cat'), the letters reach the retina of his eye and prompt electrical

stimuli to be transmitted from the optic nerve to the part of the brain responsible for processing visual information, the occipital cortex, which is situated at the back of the brain. After registration there is a comparison with previous experiences to see whether the information is new or old. If it is not new, the stimulus is reinforced and consigned to long-term memory. If it is new, it is distinguished and categorised and its relationship to other visual shapes is noted. If this new stimulus is again encountered within a few weeks, it will be reinforced and considered important enough to be sent to the long-term memory banks.

Similarly, when the word 'cat' is heard, it causes electrical changes in the auditory nerve which are then transmitted to the part of the brain responsible for processing verbal information. This is situated on the sides of the brain in the temporal lobes where registration also takes place. Thereafter, the auditory cortex determines whether the information is new or old. The same process, as with the visual stimulus, is then put into train.

The human brain has developed an area of cortex that (as well as the neocortex) is peculiar to humankind only. This is the so-called integrative cortex, an area of the brain where information from separate types of input (for example, visual, auditory, et cetera) can be brought together so that the various elements of a particular experience can be integrated. To illustrate this, you already know what a cat, for example, looks like. Therefore, whenever you read the word 'cat' this stimulus is integrated with the sound of the word and a composite picture, involving both sight and sound, brings to mind the visual image of a cat.

There is another neural system by which information can be relayed to the brain which is referred to as the tactile-kinaesthetic system. This refers to the changes we feel in pressure, touch and temperature through our skin and muscles. This information is taken up to the part of the brain which processes and registers this type of stimulus, the parietal lobes situated at the top sides of the brain. These areas allow us to perceive changes in texture, shape, solidity, and so on, which would give form to the cat mentioned above.

Therefore, if a person has stroked and felt a cat, heard its crying, seen the word 'cat' and heard the word 'cat', these separate bits of information can be correlated to form a whole concept of 'cat'. It is this integrative ability that allows us to develop symbols, a necessary step for the development of speech and language. In people with ADD, this integrative ability is less effective, and just why is discussed at page 38.

In these processes, we can see a certain organisation of learning. Information acquired through our sensory organs (eyes, ears, skin and muscles) is then focused upon and retained. It is then sent up to the processing units such as the visual and auditory cortices, where it is analysed and perceived and later sent to the integrative cortex for integration with other forms of input. The final stage is one of comprehension and conceptualisation, which involves the entire brain. The richness with which the nerve cells in all the different areas of the brain are connected to each other, as well as the total amount of these nerve cells, is a special feature of our intellect and intelligence.

This hierarchy of learning consists of a sequence of events that link up to each other but are separate functions of different parts of the nervous system. The first link in the chain is that of the end-organs such as the eyes and ears. As soon as information impinges upon these end-organs, it has to be attended to. We need to hold it in our minds long enough for the information to be held in our short-term memory banks. It can then be sent up to the processing units of the brain, the visual and auditory cortices, where it is analysed and perceived. After processing and reinforcement so that the information is stored in our long-term memory, integration occurs and the information is ready for comprehension and conceptualisation. The hierarchy that exists is as follows:

- sensory end-organ contact
- attention
- short-term memory
- perception
- reinforcement
- long-term memory
- integration
- conceptualisation.

When a person initiates an original idea of his own, that idea is first conceived in the motor part of the cerebral cortex, which is responsible for organising motor activity. Once the idea has been conceived, the frontal cortex draws upon information from the other sensory modalities by means of the integrative cortex. Here a set of instructions is formulated and transmitted to the end-organs of the motor system, such as the hands for handwriting, vocal chords for speech and general muscle movement for whole body activity (i.e., body language). The hierarchy now follows an order that runs in reverse to that of information gathering:

- conceptualisation
- integration
- long-term memory
- muscle group identification
- short-term memory
- attention
- contraction of individual muscle groups.

It is through speech, handwriting and whole body language that we communicate with our fellow human beings. Only by means of these motor systems can we show people that we have understood them or communicate an idea of our own. It is therefore essential that these systems function properly.

COGNITION AND INTEGRATION AND ADD

It is now clear that the processes involved in reading and writing are many and varied. They involve cognitive skills, which are not only elaborate but elaborately interconnected. People with ADD have a dysfunction in one or more of these cognitive skills and therefore have to circumvent this disadvantage in order to acquire or convey information. Clearly, therefore, they not only have more difficulty in processing information, but also take much longer to acquire and convey it. For these reasons, such people use more energy because when they process a set of information they require more nerve cells than other people do. As a result, the processes of reading and writing are tiring for them and often quite unrewarding. The natural inclination for people with ADD is to avoid reading and writing.

In addition, when they read they often have difficulty with left-to-right eye movement because of their poor motor ability and problems with concentration. Reading is often painstaking as they must pay attention to every word separately and cannot read in context or do speed reading where key words are focused on, instead of the whole sentence. This slows down the whole process and it often takes these people two or three times longer to read a page than the general population does.

People with ADD also have some difficulty with writing due to their inability to co-ordinate the small muscles of their hands and fingers. These people frequently have stilted handwriting due to the inappropriate or immature pencil grip that they develop; they tend to press very hard on the paper to achieve some form of stability and control over the writing. This extra pressure on the paper further constricts the flow and speed of the handwriting. The difficulty with handwriting compounds the problems they have with expressing ideas and contributes further to the truncation of their written work.

HOW TO IMPROVE YOUR READING AND WRITING SKILLS

How do you overcome these difficulties? When reading, make an effort to obtain literature that is well presented with large clear print. Books should be as short as possible and their chapters brief or broken up into sections. 'Chunking', or breaking up information into smaller sections, is a vital exercise for coping with many aspects of ADD. Generally, people with ADD are overwhelmed by problems that are presented in their entirety — more so than other people are. However, when those problems are broken down into components, they can be successfully resolved. This works for reading as well as it does for overcoming anxiety or disorganisation. When reading you should, therefore, choose books that have their information broken up into smaller sub-sections, whether they are fiction or non-fiction. The same applies for information that has to be learned for advancing your career; it should be visually attractive and broken up. There should be as many photographic illustrations as possible, because these not only break up the written work but also highlight important points.

Most people with ADD are better visual learners than they are verbal learners and, because of associated specific learning difficulties, this is in many cases a relative strength. Should this include you, make sure that any information that must be read has a visual component to complement the verbal content. Emphasise key words and other essential aspects of the text with highlighters and other visual aids.

As far as your handwriting is concerned, consult an occupational therapist for exercises to improve your hand-writing skills. Improving your pencil-grip and learning techniques in fluency and letter-formation are good starting-points. However, even with therapeutic steps such as these, many people with the disorder still experience problems with their handwriting. If this is your predicament, determine whether some form of typewriting would improve the situation. As most people with ADD are better as visual learners, the use of a keyboard often relieves them of the task of retaining the information they have to convey. It also avoids the difficulty of the fine-motor co-ordination skills involved in handwriting. I have seen young adults double their marks in university and college as a result of transferring from handwriting to keyboard skills — it is certainly a facility you should explore.

A few people recommend using secretarial services, where information can be dictated and then set out by a person who does not have ADD. This may be feasible for some but too costly or impractical for others.

Acquiring functional reading and writing skills is particularly crucial to any successful study or career, but will also affect your social and personal life. These skills will give you access to your literate environment and enable you to better comprehend the daily events that occur around you through reading newspapers, journals and magazines. Being better informed will improve your communication skills as you become more confident in contributing to discussions. Should you be required to communicate your ideas in a written form, you will be able to do so. All this will enhance your self-esteem and self-confidence, both in work and play.

Developing the skills of chunking, highlighting, visualising and word-processing, which are often forced upon people with ADD early in life, will in many cases put them a jump ahead of their peers. If you haven't yet incorporated these techniques into your learning skills, you can always begin.

KEY POINTS

- Many people with ADD are reluctant readers and writers.
- Reading and writing involve processes of integration. For example, when we read a passage, information passes from our eyes to the optical nerve, and then to the occipital cortex where it is registered and compared with existing information. If the new information is the same as an existing memory, it is consigned to long-term memory. If not, it is distinguished and categorised and its relationship to other information noted. This integrative ability is less effective in people with ADD.
- The hierarchy of learning involves: sensory end-organ contact; attention; short-term memory; perception; reinforcement; long-term memory; integration; and conceptualisation. When we initiate an idea of our own, this process is reversed.
- People with ADD have a dysfunction in one or more of the cognitive skills (listed in the previous point) necessary for reading and writing. They have more difficulty in processing information and take much longer to acquire and convey it.
- These people require more energy to process information because they use more nerve cells than those without the disorder, and as a result find the process of reading and writing very tiring.
- Also, their poor motor co-ordination causes problems with left-to-right eye movement and achieving an effective grip on their pen or pencil.

KEY POINTS (continued)

- Strategies to help you overcome these problems include: reading books with large print and lots of chapters; breaking up information into smaller sections; and taking up writing lessons or buying a typewriter.

CHAPTER SEVEN

HYPERACTIVITY

...there are days when I feel I cannot sit still.

Winston Churchill in a letter to his mother.

I want to be up and doing and cannot bear inaction or routine.

Winston Churchill, again to his mother.

The Bart Simpson of today is potentially the Kerry Packer of tomorrow, is a startling but often true statement. It is well known that many children with ADD have boundless energy. Unfortunately, their immaturity makes it very difficult for them to focus and direct this energy, and it is often unstructured and unproductive. Hyperactive children are stimulated by a stream of stimuli throughout the day, which makes them constantly change their focus of energy accordingly.

Hyperactive children are referred to by teachers and parents as dynamos who never come to rest. They are frequently in trouble because they do not leave things that are meant to be left, and do not do the things that they are meant to do. A frequent comment from parents of a hyperactive child is 'if only he would spend one quarter of his energy doing the things that he is supposed to do, he would be extraordinarily successful'.

Hyperactive children appear to have an immaturity in one of the nuclei in the diencephalon of the brain — the nucleus accumbens. Because of its dysfunction, they are unable to switch off their generators and consequently keep on the move all day, in all directions. However, they fail to perform tasks with consistent success, and tend to do a hundred and one things that remain uncompleted.

These symptoms continue throughout adolescence, which is punctuated by increasing bouts of hypoactivity (the opposite of hyperactivity) and lethargy. It is often quite perplexing how hyperactive adolescents have periods of ceaseless energy and zeal only to be followed by times of flaccidity and indolence. The older these children become, the greater are the periods of hypoactivity.

As a young adult, the dangers of the hyperactivity are the bouts of superfluous undirected energy and the periods of indolence, also undirected. Eventually, there will be an improvement in both these aspects, but often only as late as the third or fourth decades of life.

The earlier hyperactive adults can harness their great resource, the sooner they can compete successfully in the workplace. Whereas in children the extra energy is a disadvantage (they have difficulty in concentrating on single tasks and completing them, adults are more able to do so), for adults it is often a distinct advantage; they can manage much more work in a day than their peers can. It is evident that hyperactive people push themselves harder and are often referred to as 'workaholics'.

These people are able to do more things in a shorter time as they seem to have limitless stamina for work and can use this to advantage in their career opportunities. The problems for them, however, are the periods of diminished activity and performance. It seems that these occur more frequently in the recreational situation than at work.

HOW TO MANAGE YOUR HYPERACTIVITY

If you are a hyperactive adult what you must do is recognise the advantage of the increased energy levels and harness them. You would then, for instance, be able to hold down a day job and study at night or perhaps moonlight in a second job. You would also have a greater capacity than most people have to work over weekends and after hours. These attributes, highly valued by employers, are seen as an indication of a person's commitment and dedication. However, for you the extra workload is a biological necessity. You more than likely find that you need to work to get rid of your excess energy levels, otherwise you become frustrated. Be careful not to let your surplus of energy make you frustrated, as this can have a negative influence on your life.

Frustrated overactive adults often direct their energies into antisocial activities and are at high risk of becoming involved in petty or major crime. They do not realise that their increased energy levels are propelling them into activities that they would otherwise prefer not to pursue. However, many of these people have left school with poor scholastic levels and damaging testimonials from their headmasters, and thus find their progress in the normal workplace is often thwarted. They are, therefore, not able to obtain the positions that are commensurate with their intelligence and abilities. As this realisation dawns upon them, they become increasingly frustrated and start to divert their energies in areas where there is less resistance. As a result, they become involved with other people (often of a similar nature, that is with some sort of conduct disorder) who have taken to small-time crime and in this way start the downhill path to organised crime and possible imprisonment.

If hyperactive people are alerted to the dangers of their condition at an early stage, and if their academic disadvantages are given remedial treatment, they can be encouraged and persuaded to direct their efforts in a more productive and socially acceptable manner. I am of the firm belief that there is a large group of people who have great skills and talents to offer, but who are prevented from doing so because they are already locked in to a lifestyle that is not mainstream. I have already touched on one of the major causes of these difficulties — the poor acquisition of reading, writing and arithmetic. If these children are recognised earlier, their learning disabilities can be corrected and they can be encouraged to pursue orthodox careers. Adults with this difficulty should be made aware of this condition and should seek the services of a good psychologist or physician to help them co-ordinate a programme that channels their natural abilities properly.

Those who are already in a suitable career should try hard to control their energies outside work. The inability to conduct their social lives with a proper sense of balance frequently tends to prevent these people from developing this aspect of their lives. It is as if they are unable to turn off their generator switches when they come home. They tend to continue being very high-powered in their leisure time and take up a variety of sports as outlets for their excess energies. This overflow can be very useful — it can be channelled constructively by working around the home or spending some time with their families. However, families of hyperactive people make the frequent complaint that they never seem able to slow down and relax. When they go on holiday these people are still moving at 'hyperspeed'. They seem compelled to do everything almost within the first day of their holiday, and are constantly seeking other outlets for their high activity levels.

If you are hyperactive it is important for you to be aware that there are times when you must reduce your energy levels, not only to conserve energy but also to tune in to people who do not have such stamina. This is often hard to do, but is vital for successful social integration.

When an overactive person comes home from work in the evening, there should be a period where he switches over from the highly-paced daily activities into a slower social situation. This could be done by reading the paper, watching the news, or having a drink with his partner. Should he feel the need to go out in the evening, it should be limited to one activity. Arranging to do several things in one evening will again lead to the hyped-up state experienced during the day, and is a recipe for disaster. Over the weekends his leisure activities should be fairly structured, but again with the emphasis on keeping them lower than the workplace levels. There is no doubt that because of their high energy levels, these people contribute much to the community. They are often on local school committees or councils and frequently are involved in running charitable organisations. These are other useful means by which you can channel your excess energies, but you should also keep these activities under control to minimise the risk of neglecting your family and friends.

By keeping aware of the resource potential of excess activity levels, and by properly channelling these activities in the workplace, in the home and in social settings, you can not only be more successful, but can also have a competitive edge over your colleagues or peers.

KEY POINTS

- Hyperactivity is a common problem in children with ADD. Unfortunately, their boundless energy is without direction and it is usually unproductive.
- For adolescents and adults, problems include bouts of undirected energy followed by periods of indolence. This feature does improve, but often not until the third or fourth decade of life.
- A secondary associated problem relates to the person who left school with poor grades due to the disorder and who finds progress in the workplace difficult. Their frustration can lead them into crime.
- Many who are in a suitable occupation find it difficult to relax at home, and constantly seek outlets for their excess energy. It is vital that these people become aware of the problem and develop ways to control it.
- The earlier hyperactive adults can harness their resources of energy, the sooner they can turn a disadvantage into an advantage. These people can push themselves more than most, and are often known as workaholics.
- By properly channelling their energy, hyperactive adults can have a competitive edge over their colleagues and peers.

CHAPTER EIGHT

IMPULSIVENESS

... I do so want you to have more discretion & judgement about spending your money. You do everything at random my Pet without thinking...

Mrs Everest, Winston Churchill's childhood nanny to Winston.

Impulsiveness is perhaps the most disabling of all the features of ADD, especially when viewed over the long term. As the person with ADD grows older, the hyperactivity diminishes and many other features become semi-manageable. However, the emotional — and especially the verbal — impulsiveness the disorder can cause continue as particularly socially disabling. Impulsiveness is the immediate response to a thought or deed without consideration of its appropriateness or consequences.

People with ADD who are hyperactive and impulsive appear to have an uncanny ability for reacting reflexively to stimuli. Their over-reactive gross-motor reflexes seem to be paralleled by their reflex reactions to various situations. They tend to make decisions on the spur of the moment after taking in the various circumstances in a fraction of a second. This faculty is often of great benefit where the decisions made are correct for they act upon them with a singlemindedness that generally ensures success.

However, many of these snap decisions are catastrophically incorrect and lead to disastrous results. These setbacks are apparently brushed aside and are not allowed to affect any future decisions. In other words, such people seldom seem to learn from past experiences and often make the same mistake several times. It is presumed that the biological cause of the impulsiveness is very likely the lack of inhibiting neurotransmitters from the neocortex upon the stimuli from the diencephalon (see Chapter 3 if you need to refresh your memory of these physiological processes).

We have seen in Chapter 3 how in the learning process information is collected from the environment via the sensory system, perceived by the brain, stored for later recall and acted upon via the motor system. For people with ADD and impulsiveness, impulsiveness intervenes at each of the major stages in this process and may, therefore, be subdivided into four categories: sensory (or emotional); intellectual (or cognitive); physical (or motor); and verbal (or linguistic) impulsiveness.

EMOTIONAL

Emotionally impulsive people tend to sum up other people very rapidly upon first meeting. They make emotional decisions about the other person's conduct, body language, verbal communication and actions far too quickly. As a result they often miss vital and important clues in their contact with others, and this may lead them to misjudge other people's personalities. They tend to make impetuous assumptions about how other people feel toward them, based on misinterpretations of their body language. When this tendency is added to self-esteem difficulties and inflexibility (other characteristics of ADD) these people are in danger of jumping to the wrong conclusion about someone they meet. This can often develop into general paranoia about people.

It is widely recognised that impulsive people are likely to have a distinct pleasure-seeking or even thrill-seeking aspect to their personalities. They are therefore very much at risk of substance abuse to satisfy this thirst for emotional satisfaction. Without the necessary check mechanisms of the higher neocortex upon the diencephalon, such people are at risk of becoming addicted to drugs or alcohol later on. Alcoholism is common in families where ADD is coupled with hyperactivity.

INTELLECTUAL

The rapid decision-making of intellectually impulsive people has already been referred to. It seems that these people collate very little information before making a decision. They give little thought to alternatives to any chosen course of action.

Academically, these people are generally prone to making wrong assumptions from written language because their impulsiveness makes them pick out one or two key words from a sentence and then make their decisions and proceed to act on insufficient information. It is almost as if they have blind spots that prevent them from picking up all the relevant bits and properly processing them. For example, many impulsive students misread examination questions and embark on the wrong answers because they do not give themselves time to analyse the full question.

We see children with this problem making errors in addition and subtraction as they often impetuously leave out or misplace numbers that should be borrowed or carried over to the next column. After that, they seldom take the time or effort to check their calculations. This lack of ability to check and compare details is an essential feature of impulsiveness, and persists into adulthood.

VERBAL

What is probably the most disconcerting aspect of impulsiveness is verbal impetuosity. Many such people tend to verbalise their thoughts and ideas without first giving them due reflection. These people will often think of something funny and relate it without thinking that it could distress the company. We all probably know someone who is prone to telling jokes that have their punchlines based upon religious or physical differences. The impulsive joke-teller, however, fails to assess his audience and invariably one of these people falls into the category he is lampooning.

However, this feature is also quite disabling in a career situation. For example, a person with ADD is more likely to express his dislike of certain office procedures to his superior than to control his impetuosity and offer diplomatic criticism by way of constructive comment. This can result in problems with the progression of his career and social contact in the workplace.

PHYSICAL

This is the impulsiveness that is so prominent amongst hyperactive children with ADD. They are the children who are likely to run across the road without looking to see if any cars are approaching. They are inclined to run along high walls or rooftops and even jump out of high trees without thinking about hurting themselves.

Although this tendency does lessen with age and some learned experience does take hold in their cognitive functioning, many adults with ADD still experience some physical impulsiveness. I know of one incident where a young adult was attracted by his father's revolver and, trying to see how it would function he pulled the trigger without further thought. Unfortunately, his brother was in the path of the gun and was shot in the stomach. On later questioning, the young man said that he had not even thought about the consequences, he just wanted to see how the gun worked.

I can think of my own experience as a young trainee pilot in the air force. I was doing a reconnaissance flight and came upon a farmer ploughing his field with some oxen. Apart from the novelty of the scene, I thought immediately that it would be great fun to pass fairly low over the farmer and see what happened. Without much ado I descended. I then pulled up immediately afterwards into the sky and looked back to see the results of my handiwork. Of course, the oxen had dislodged from the plough and were travelling in one direction and the farmer in the other. However, I forgot to look at my air speed and when I did so I was perilously close to the speed at which the aircraft would have stalled since I was so close to the ground; if I *had* stalled, it would have been fatal.

These are just a few examples of the kinds of physical reactions to an impulsive thought process that are features so characteristic of ADD.

HOW TO COPE WITH IMPULSIVENESS
It is clear from all this that impulsiveness is far-reaching. It can often be an advantage because of the rapidity with which

these people can link up the essential processes of decision-making. However, pausing to reflect and consider the alternatives before taking the final decision would greatly enhance these people's ability not only to perform appropriately, but also to compete successfully with others in the workplace. It would also improve their social skills and make them more emotionally satisfied and happy. They would also be at far less risk for injury and physical danger, especially in situations such as driving a vehicle. We all know of the impulsive young male ADD who drives too close and too fast behind the car in front of him without giving thought to the possible consequences of having to stop suddenly.

I suggest using the subliminal method to overcome this tendency. I put pieces of paper with the words 'think then act' everywhere in my bedroom, including at the foot of my bed, in my briefcase, inside my locker door, on my bicycle, on the dashboard of my car. Eventually the message sank in and I am pleased to say that nowadays I pause before acting impulsively.

With a full understanding of this potentially disastrous characteristic, you can reduce the risks of impulsiveness and allow the positive features to become the advantages that they undoubtedly are. Apart from my above suggestion and bitter experience teaching you to think before you act, drug therapy has the best effect upon this aspect of ADD. Drug therapy is discussed in detail at Chapter 14.

KEY POINTS

- Impulsiveness is a disabling, long-term feature of ADD.
- Impulsiveness is the immediate response to a thought or deed without consideration of its appropriateness or consequences.
- Features of impulsiveness include: making decisions on the spur of the moment; and making the same mistake several times (as these people do not think on and learn from past experiences).
- There are four categories of impulsiveness:
  Emotional: includes summing up others very rapidly and making false assumptions about them. This can lead to paranoia. Their thirst for emotional satisfaction puts these people at risk of substance abuse.
  Intellectual: Includes misinterpretation of facts (for example, misreading an exam question because they don't give themselves time to analyse it properly), and a lack of ability to check details.
  Verbal: Includes speaking without thought to what is said. This feature can be disabling in social and career situations.
  Physical: Acting without thinking.
- Strategies to help you overcome this problem include: pausing and reflecting on alternative responses; and placing a sign that reads 'Think then Act' on your bedroom wall.
- Impulsiveness can be a positive feature — the ability to make a quick decision and see it through is a quality required of leaders.

CHAPTER NINE

ORGANISATION

...but his forgetfulness, carelessness, unpunctuality, and irregularity in every way, have really been so serious, that I ... sometimes think he cannot help it.

Henry Davidson (assistant master at Harrow) to
Lady Randolph Churchill, Winston's mother.

Every second of the day the human brain is bombarded with information which it has to register and analyse. This learning experience is referred to in Chapter 6 as the hierarchy of learning. However, for this learning to occur all the information from the chaos of external stimuli has to be organised and meaning extracted.

Just as the process of learning follows a certain route, so too is there a certain order in the way input is arranged and categorised. First, stimuli from the environment are registered; then they are sorted, according to whether they are familiar or new. New stimuli are eventually reinforced if they are presented again, and are then put into our long-term memory. At this stage the information becomes available almost automatically without much conscious effort.

The brain's organisational processes eventually allow bits of trivia to be processed automatically so that we react to them at a subconscious level. For example, from infancy we learn to brush our teeth in the morning and at night, as well as to comb our hair. Eventually, these actions become so routine and automatic that we frequently do them without thinking and often cannot remember if we have performed them that day. The various organisational processes involved in performing tasks have become so habitual that they require very little input from the higher processes of our cognitive skills.

This faculty of the brain to automatise so much information leaves it free for more important cognitive functions such as language, communication, abstract reasoning and conceptualisation.

ORGANISATION AND ADD

The part of the brain that is affected by ADD plays a significant role in the development of organisational and planning skills. Therefore people with ADD have significant problems with organising their environment, both internally and externally. They find it very difficult to arrange their internal thoughts into efficient, useful trains of logic. These difficulties with internal organisation are reflected by signs of external disorder. People with ADD have great problems in sorting out their daily activities efficiently, and often repeat tasks because they do not plan ahead. In many cases they omit to perform certain functions as they were not included in the organisational framework for the day, or else are forgotten.

In childhood, these people are often the banes of their mothers' existences. They are the children who find it very difficult to get their school things together in the morning and tend to dawdle or potter around aimlessly. Invariably they do not have the books, homework or equipment required for school that day. Notes from school are generally forgotten and forthcoming activities are not properly prepared for. Their bedrooms are usually in a mess.

This inability to order the environment continues throughout adolescence, often becoming pervasive by adulthood. At the root of these difficulties in organisation is the inability to plan ahead and to maintain fairly firm schedules of activity.

IMPROVING YOUR ORGANISATIONAL SKILLS

Establishing the principles of routine, regularity and repetition are important for the child with ADD, and also for the adult. Unless adults with ADD are able to develop a consistent, strict schedule for doing things at certain times in the day and backing this up with physical aids such as lists or diaries, they will invariably be lost. Their predicament is compounded by the fact that they often have superfluous energy levels and take on more than other people do. They therefore feel that they have the energy to achieve so much more in life, but find this is handicapped by their poor organisation of routine, which in turn restricts their time for concentrating on things that require more of their higher cognitive thinking.

To overcome these organisational difficulties you need to do three vital things:

1. Arrange the day into a steady schedule, and if necessary, divide it into timeslots, allowing one for each task or activity. It is important to try to keep to this 'diary' schedule for all daily activities. It helps you to see how much time is available in the day and how much can be achieved without stretching your resources or those of your colleagues.
2. Make lists or notes. Jotting down points through the day helps you to keep track of and finish your tasks which would otherwise be forgotten, lost or unfinished.
3. Plan well ahead of time. When activities are planned, there is more time to rectify errors and to include extra activities or material if required. I must stress the importance of

developing the faculty of planning as this eliminates many errors that inappropriate time-allocation and forgetfulness can cause.

Quite clearly, as a person with ADD, you must make a special effort to develop organisational skills. However, once you are aware of this and can put into train a set of strategies to compensate for these difficulties, you will often have a distinct advantage over your colleagues. For example, by arranging your daily programme into an organised and comprehensible pattern, you are free to perform other more challenging tasks and in this way can harness your own talents more successfully. By adhering to routine, repetition and regularity, you will be able to perform with consistency, calm and control instead of the previous random style and in so doing, reduce the stress placed upon you in your daily life.

KEY POINTS

- Our ability to do things automatically (such as brushing our teeth) leaves us free to concentrate on more cognitive functions, such as language, communication, reasoning and conceptualisation.
- The part of the brain responsible for organisation is affected by ADD. People with the disorder therefore find it difficult to organise their internal and external environments.
- These people have problems with logic, organising their daily activities and keeping their rooms tidy.
- Strategies to help you overcome the problem include: establishing regularity, routine and repetition in tasks; scheduling what needs to be done that day, as well as long-term planning.

CHAPTER TEN

SELF-ESTEEM

Perhaps my book may be a financial success. Mind you write and say nice things to me about it. Tell me what parts you like. I love praise. It is delicious.

Winston Churchill to his mother.

'No, David, you can't play with us this time. You can't throw and catch a ball and you can't kick straight. None of us wants you in this game.'

'Louise, you just won't understand the way this works. We know that you can't read properly, or something like that, and that's just going to slow us down. Sorry, but perhaps next time.'

There are many people with ADD who have had comments like these thrown at them when they were at school or playing in the neighbourhood. These comments go to the very heart of what is probably a major dysfunction in ADD: the low self-esteem or poor self-image that these people develop in childhood and adolescence. Thus, potential weapons in the battle with the onslaught of adult life are severely weakened by ADD, and this has lifelong implications which are detailed later in this chapter.

What is self-esteem? Self-esteem is our mind's-eye image of our sum total of physical attributes, athletic skills, academic abilities and social skills. It is how we portray ourselves to ourselves, and how we feel we are perceived by other people in our surroundings. It is, in other words, a mental identikit that we carry every day in our subconscious and conscious mind — one that gives us an almost minute-by-minute, blow-by-blow account of how we are developing, achieving and integrating with society.

The neocortex (the part of the brain that is involved in ADD) also plays a major role in the development of our self-concept and, in turn, our self-confidence. As it is immature and dysfunctioning in people with the disorder, their self-esteem cannot therefore develop appropriately in childhood and adolescence, and will be deficient when they enter adulthood. These people have a disadvantage to start with, in that they cannot develop a self-image that truly reflects their natural abilities. Most, if not all, have a poorly developed self-esteem that affects their whole attitude to life.

This problem with self-esteem is compounded by their inability to develop the skills that come naturally to their peers. As already discussed, children with ADD experience problems with their attention, memory and perception which make learning difficult for them. They may also have speech development problems which make them obvious targets for teasing and derision, both in the classroom and outside. They may have trouble with co-ordination that makes them clumsy and bumble-footed, and with fine-motor tasks or with catching balls and throwing them. It is especially the speech and co-ordination difficulties that give them a high profile — not necessarily the type they would like. Many of these children are hyperactive and impulsive, which further contributes to their image as someone who is different and inferior.

The lack of ability to improve these skills and functions reinforces the poor self-esteem, so that people with ADD doubt their self-worth throughout childhood and adolescence. When they enter adulthood they are unlikely to regard themselves as people who can perform well and achieve successfully in life. Their self-esteem is so fragile that it only lasts from one success to the next. Where most people will derive satisfaction for a long time from an achievement or encouraging comment and use that to shore up and improve their self-esteem, the person with ADD does not retain that satisfaction, it seldom lasts for more than a day or two. It seems that they need to be constantly reassured that they are people of worth and ability and are achieving appropriately. I have seen many people with ADD who achieve extremely well, but even when they do, they find it difficult to think highly of themselves and seem to need constant reward and compliments to keep themselves going.

In adulthood, the poor self-esteem adversely affects not only these people's social interaction, but also the progress of their career. Because they doubt themselves, they find that they do not have the necessary self-confidence to go for the opportunities the workplace offers.

Many of us who have ADD will recall how in school we made sure that we were as invisible as possible in the classroom. We were concerned that at some stage the teacher would pick on us to answer a question or stand up and state our opinion in front of the class. Although in many cases we may have known the answer, we lacked the self-confidence and self-esteem to respond appropriately and were especially fearful of being laughed at by the rest of the class. It is this memory that we carry over into adulthood so that we find ourselves not only doubting our abilities, but also fearful of being derided at work or in social settings. For this reason, we prefer to work in situations where we only have to deal with people one at a time or, at most, in small groups. In this kind of setting we have a certain amount of control over events and can speak individually to others without the fear of the rest of the group mobilising against us. As you may have assumed, people with self-esteem difficulties related to ADD tend to develop a certain paranoia; they are so concerned about what other people think of them that they suspiciously imagine situations that do not exist.

That is the negative aspect of the self-esteem difficulty in ADD. How do people with the condition go about compensating for it and possibly using it to their advantage?

IMPROVING YOUR SELF-ESTEEM

I recall when I was a medical student and had experienced difficulty comparing my abilities favourably with those of colleagues, I took a course of action that I have found successful ever since.

I remember that when we went on hospital ward rounds I always stood at the back of the group so that the lecturer or professor wouldn't recognise me or see the name on my badge. I thought that in that way he wouldn't be able to call me forward either to examine a patient or discuss some particular disorder. I realised that this was preventing me from taking an active part in analysing the work at hand, and from making my own conclusions. I therefore relied more and more upon other people's opinions and upon what I read in textbooks.

To counteract this lack of confidence I decided to choose an area of study that generally baffled virtually all medical students and doctors. I thought if I could direct my energies to understanding certain aspects of neurology better than other people around me, I would be able to speak with more authority in a group because I would be less likely to be contradicted by others. As a result, I spent most of my spare time studying, working on and discussing aspects of neurology.

Neurology is traditionally considered to be a very difficult and abstruse part of medicine because it is not easily studied directly (as other organs are) since the brain is very conveniently protected by this hard shell. To my delight I realised that the further I delved into this subject, the more logical it became and the more interesting. Often that is the case — when you have a particular weakness it becomes a strength after persistent exercising and support. For instance, a tennis player who has a weak backhand will find that opponents play to that backhand all the time, so that the tennis player gets the match practice he needs; eventually his backhand not only improves but becomes a particular strength in his array of strokes.

With my concentration upon neurology, I was able to make this aspect a strength out of what was initially a decided weakness. On a subsequent ward round a neurological disorder was being discussed and I was able to volunteer my knowledge and was called forward to discuss the patient in front of the other students. This kept recurring and eventually I was accepted by the other members of the ward round as the person to consult over any neurological condition. In this way I not only developed an ability that was of great interest and use to me later in life, but I was also able to compensate for my inabilities in other areas.

One of the major requirements of a young doctor is to be

able to listen to the heart, hear murmurs between the heart sounds, and detect whether there is any difficulty or impending disease. I must confess that I have very rarely heard heart murmurs and I doubt if I ever will. It is a faculty you either have or do not have. There are many other aspects in the medical examination which also require the development of certain skills. My growing expertise in neurology shielded me from the exposure in areas in which I was weak, allowing me time to develop them where I could and improve my general medical examination skills.

The point I am trying to make is that to overcome a self-esteem problem in the workplace you should focus on an area that is not any colleague's speciality. You should then develop this as a particular interest, to the point of expertise. In this way a weakness can become a strength and the strength can eventually help to improve other skills and earn the respect of colleagues. I have used this ploy on many occasions since my student days and found it to be particularly successful.

This is just one technique for improving your self-esteem. A similar strategy can be used in the social environment, where you need to engage socially with people. You should develop some expertise in one or two special topics so that you can discuss them in detail and with a certain amount of authority at social gatherings. Eventually, people will acknowledge your expertise and listen more readily to your opinions in these areas. In this way you will become known as a person who has skills and insight worth consulting.

It is also useful to keep a list of your sporting, social and academic successes. Reading through them from time to time you will not only bolster your self-esteem, especially if you are going through a rough patch, but they will refresh your mind about why they were so successful. Consequently, a life that appears to be one of valleys may be changed into a landscape of peaks.

Reading about the other aspects of ADD discussed in this book (such as impulsiveness, memory and concentration problems, poor organisational skills, etc.) might also help to improve your self-esteem. However, singling out and developing an unpopular or neglected area, to the point of making it your own special strength, is a strategy that is enduring and successful, and one that I highly recommend both to children and adults with ADD.

KEY POINTS

- The low self-esteem of many people with ADD develops in childhood. As children, these people were often teased for their inability to keep up with their peers, for their poor co-ordination, or for speech problems.

- Poor self-esteem affects their whole attitude to adult life. Regarding work, for example, these people do not have the confidence to take up opportunities and fear derision if they do make an effort.

- Strategies to help you overcome the problem include: studying a subject relevant to your work that is not any colleague's speciality so that others will find your knowledge useful; socially, develop some expertise on one or two topics so that you can discuss them with some authority; make a list of your achievements and read through them from time to time.

CHAPTER ELEVEN

PERSONALITY TRAITS

*Take care of yourself & work well & keep out of scrapes & don't flare up
so easily!!!*

Fanny, Duchess of Marlborough,
to her grandson Winston Churchill.

There are some distinct personality traits that are part of
ADD, but not all of them necessarily occur in every person
with this condition. Most of them are negative characteristics
(such as frustration, anger and anxiety) and should be reduced
as much as possible. Others, such as inflexibility and
aggression, are largely negative qualities but can often be
converted to become benefits.

FRUSTRATION
Most parents of hyperactive children know that one of the
most difficult features these children have to contend with
is a low frustration threshold. They seem to have a low
tolerance for anything that obstructs or thwarts their desires.
This problem often continues into adulthood, and has
repercussions in both physical (behavioural) and intellectual
(academic) situations.

These people seem to have only two modes of dealing with
either situation. First, they would try to physically remove
the obstacle, often in a frenzy of anger. This is an example
of the physical frustration. Secondly, if they are frustrated

by an intellectual exercise (such as a task at school or a job assigned in their workplace) the natural inclination would be to avoid it and try something easier, or to ignore the exercise altogether.

It is therefore clear that if you have this problem, one of the main methods of contending with frustration is to avoid the frustrating stimulus in the first place. If the frustrating stimulus cannot be removed or avoided, then acknowledging that your low frustration threshold as something you need to control will help you to avoid acting too impulsively. Also, try to develop the habit of anticipating situations or social encounters which experience has taught you are fraught with frustration. This will help you to be ready to deal with your response. Apart from drug therapy, which is referred to later in this book, this is really the only way to countering the frustrations that occur in day-to-day living.

ANGER

One of the most negative features of ADD is anger, which can often flare up without reason. People with this tendency seem to boil over and often have enormously passionate responses to relatively minor incidents. Their anger is very typically characterised by its rapid onset and decline. During such an attack people often lose control of their emotions, and many crimes of passion are due to this feature. Fathers who have ADD very often respond unreasonably to misdemeanours by their children because they cannot control their anger, and the punishment meted out is seldom appropriate to the misdeed.

Again, the best way to cope with such a tendency to anger

is to be aware of it and remove or avoid potential stimulus that experience has taught you will provoke it. Removal of the offending stimulus not only helps to prevent the anger from increasing, but also allows you time to regain control of your emotions and view things a little bit more objectively. If the situation is unavoidable, remember that people with ADD tend to over-react impulsively to situations. Try to prepare yourself by 'prethinking' through potentially upsetting situations. Here again, drug therapy is also very useful in helping to control angry outbursts.

ANXIETY

Research has shown that the most common personality trait in adults with ADD is that of anxiety. It can lead to incapacitating levels of apprehension and nervousness, especially in new situations. These people are the great worriers in life and because they are so concerned about the unknown, they need as much information as possible about any new places, people or positions they might encounter.

People with ADD and anxiety tend to be tense and this affects their moods throughout the day. They find it difficult to relax even when asleep. The anxiety eventually infiltrates not only their inner selves, but also their outer environment, affecting their career, social interactions and family relationships.

One way to deal with this trait is to take time to analyse the cause of your anxiety. Then break the problem up into components, so that something that once seemed huge and intimidating, now appears manageable. Once this is done (it is referred to by educationists as 'chunking') each little bit can be successfully tackled on its own and this alleviates the anxiety.

Another strategy is to familiarise yourself with new situations or environments before they are met full-on. If you have just been successful in your application for a new job, take some time after hours, when there are fewer people in the workplace, to visit the premises and familiarise yourself with its structural features and with the routine of travelling there and home again. When there are fewer people it is often easier to make some acquaintances, and this makes the first few days a little easier.

I have found in my practice that relaxation therapy is sometimes very useful for people with this aspect of ADD. A visit to a good psychologist who can apply not only relaxation but even perhaps some hypnotherapy may also help.

INFLEXIBILITY
This seems to be another characteristic of people with ADD who are also hyperactive. Their inflexibility is not only intellectual but emotional. They find that once they have made a decision there is no going back, and it is very difficult for such people to adapt in the face of altered circumstances. Their faculty for compromise is weak and once embarked on a certain direction, there is little chance of them deviating from it.

These people also show a certain amount of intolerance and impatience towards others, and to any ideas or alternative courses of action that would upset their own decision. Their inflexibility appears to be a strategy that they employ to help them cope with the apparent chaos of their internal and external lives. It is, therefore, a survival technique for them, and is often quite successful.

Inflexibility can produce a certain amount of useful single-mindedness; for example, when a decision is made it will be pursued until that goal is achieved. Such tenacity is generally much appreciated by employers. However, inflexibility should be tempered so that in the initial stages of decision making alternatives can be considered and the best course chosen. Thereafter, tenacity can only be an advantage, and it often brings reward. A habit of considering alternatives takes a long time to acquire, but should be worked at steadily as the potential rewards are considerable.

AGGRESSION

Aggression, like impulsiveness, can be subdivided into four subcategories: physical, emotional, verbal and intellectual.

Physical aggression is often displayed in the young child; for example, the young bully who terrorises other students. If this habit continues into adulthood, it needs to be treated, otherwise these people will always resolve their disputes with physical force.

Where the aggression is of an emotional nature, these people harass others and place enormous pressure on them until they concede to their point of view. This is something that occurs frequently in the workplace, in the form of sexual harassment; or in the home situation, where one partner emotionally browbeats another.

Verbal aggression is often more dramatic and more common than any other type of aggression, and is characterised by continual swearing or abuse with which the aggressor hopes to wear someone down. This verbal aggression must be distinguished from the emotional aggression because the latter is sometimes conveyed by body language alone, without any verbal language at all.

Intellectual aggression is seen in people who are very determined to achieve goals, especially in the workplace, and who will stop at nothing to achieve them. They tend to ride over colleagues and will use anything or anyone of advantage to them. They are determined to be first in line for accolades or rewards and are often very challenging in their dealings with colleagues.

If aggression is a feature of your ADD, one of the best methods of coping with it is to be aware of it. Certainly, a controlled amount of aggression is useful in one's career, but physical, emotional and verbal aggression should be tempered. Once you realise that naked aggression only leads to trouble and that more moderate actions are more appropriate and successful, aggression can then be put to some advantage.

KEY POINTS
- There are distinct personality traits that are a part of ADD but do not occur in every person with the disorder. These include:

  Frustration: Many with ADD have a low frustration threshold. To deal with a frustrating situation they either remove the obstacle, often in a frenzy of anger, or avoid the situation altogether. Being aware of a potentially frustrating situation and controlling your response will help.

  Anger: This tendency is characterised by its rapid onset and decline. Again, being aware of the problem, avoiding potentially difficult situations, or taking 'time-out' to regain control over your emotions will all help.

> **KEY POINTS (continued)**
>
> *Anxiety:* can lead to incapacitating levels of apprehension and nervousness. Analysing the cause of your anxiety and breaking the problem down into its components will help you to deal with it. Relaxation therapy may also help.
>
> *Inflexibility:* Once those with this problem make a decision, there is no going back. Their ability to compromise is weak, and they are often intolerant and impatient. These people often use inflexibility as a way to put order into the apparent chaos of their lives. Their singlemindedness can be an advantage; decisions will be pursued with tenacity. However, learn to temper decisions with consideration of alternatives.
>
> *Aggression:* Like impulsiveness, aggression can be subdivided into four main categories: physical, emotional, verbal and intellectual. It results in bullying, harassing, swearing, and taking advantage of others. Realise that a certain amount of controlled aggression can be useful at times but usually its energy is best directed into more appropriate responses.

CHAPTER TWELVE

SOCIAL IMPERCEPTION

...it may have been nicer & perhaps wiser to have begun by consulting me ... But I suppose experience of life will in time teach you that tact is a very essential ingredient in all things.

Lady Randolph Churchill to her son Winston.

Social interaction is an aspect of virtually all animal life. However, it is of greater complexity in the primates and is even more sophisticated in human beings. The ability of members of a species to communicate with each other in a social context is essential not only for the continuation of that species but also for the smooth integration of its members and the functioning of that society. Good social intercourse leads to a more successful homeostatic (balanced) existence.

Engaging in social intercourse may be likened to participating in a dance: the two people involved in a dance constantly read each other's movements and adjust their own accordingly. Dancing also involves a significant degree of anticipation — one partner almost second-guesses what the other is about to do and formulates his or her steps accordingly. This anticipation is crucial to well co-ordinated dancing. These abilities are also essential for proper social intercourse. In both activities, people have to be constantly aware of the thoughts of others, and anticipate any changes. As well as the verbal communication that takes place in socialisation, people have to be aware, therefore, of each other's body language.

Many people with ADD seem to have developed the skill

of social intercourse insufficiently. They are almost obtuse about changes in body language and the social cues by which people in a social context modulate each other's behaviour. People with the disorder almost seem to be living in a world of their own, unaffected by others' sensibilities. They do, of course, have mood changes too, but cannot read other people's. Here are a few examples of such social bluntness.

A middle-aged lady is planning to give a party in a few weeks, and has decided to offer some form of entertainment, such as a magician, however, she is at a loss as to how to contact such a person. After giving the matter some thought, she visits her next-door neighbour whom she has known for the last twenty years. She asks her neighbour if she knows of anyone who would fit the bill, but meanwhile fails to notice her neighbour's hurt expression at not being invited to the party, especially as mutual friends have been invited. If the party-giver had noticed her neighbour's reaction, she might have made amends.

A middle-aged, successful businessman has bought a boat and gone out on the harbour to enjoy himself. However, he returns that evening furious about the poor manners of other boat owners on the water. What he had failed to realise was that his own actions — obstructing other boats, and intimidating small craft — had led to his altercations with so many other boat owners. He was unable to comprehend that the bullying tactics that he used so successfully in business were not acceptable as boating etiquette, nor to a social setting where he was on equal terms with everyone else. He could not see that he himself was the one at fault.

The mother of one of my patients rang my secretary to make an earlier appointment for her son. Unfortunately, none was available. Without any change in the tone of her voice, she asked the secretary to rearrange things so that her son could have another patient's appointment. The fact that she was encroaching on someone else's right never occurred to her.

There are many other examples of people with ADD invading the privacy of others. Some of them think nothing of entering someone else's bedroom and examining it, or even reading other people's mail. However, when the same treatment is meted out to them, they feel terribly wronged and cry out at the injustice of it. One young man read about corruption in the police force and said that he didn't think it was a matter of much concern. He could not see the greater social implications of the actions of the corrupt police officers, but would have been greatly alarmed if he himself had been the victim.

People with social imperception caused by ADD have great difficulty in understanding, let alone accepting that certain social mores are necessary for the successful existence of a society. Only when the breakdown of these social customs affects them personally do they react. It takes them a long time to learn the fruitfulness of the teaching 'do unto others as you would have them do unto you'.

HOW TO IMPROVE YOUR SOCIAL SKILLS
This particular characteristic of ADD does not necessarily affect careers severely, but certainly affects social development. It is therefore essentially a negative feature of ADD and if this is a feature of your ADD, one of the best ways to contend with it is to be fully aware of its existence.

Monitor your behaviour and other people's reactions to what you say or do to discover when you may be acting without any regard for others. Try to put yourself in their position. Learn how to read the subtleties of verbal expression and body language which indicate how they may be feeling. This will help you to interpret better the reactions of others. Also develop a habit of thinking about the effect of what you are going to say before you say it and adjusting your comment accordingly.

All this will help you to improve your tactfulness and consideration. If you can do that, you will become a much better integrated social animal, and this will benefit all aspects of your life.

KEY POINTS

- Many people with ADD do not sufficiently develop the skill of social intercourse.
- These people are obtuse about changes in body language and the social cues by which people moderate their behaviour.
- Those with this problem can appear to be living in a world of their own, unaffected by others' sensibilities. They often offend others or invade their privacy, but cry out when the same treatment is given to them.
- Strategies to improve your social skills include: being aware of the problem, monitoring your behaviour and others' reactions to learn when you may be acting without regard for them; learning to read body language; and developing the habit of thinking about the effect of what you will say before you say it.

CHAPTER THIRTEEN

DIAGNOSIS

School was a sombre grey patch on the chart of my journey. It was an unending spell of worries that did not then seem petty, and of toil uncheered by fruition; a time of discomfort, restriction and purposeless monotony. All my contemporaries seemed in every way better adapted to the condition of our little world. They were far better at both games and at the lessons. It is not pleasant to feel oneself so completely outclassed and left behind at the very beginning of the race.

Winston Churchill's reflections upon his schooling.

The process of diagnosing ADD in adults is similar to that for children. Any differences are largely related to the fact that adults, unlike children, are not in a stage of growth and development. When children are assessed for ADD, their developing skills must be taken into account. Adults, however, have already developed their central nervous systems and most of their social and learning patterns.

In either case diagnosing ADD is still based upon the three principles of clinical examination, psychological investigation and neurophysiological measurement.

1. Clinical examination relies upon examining a person's childhood and adolescent history for telltale symptoms of ADD. The physician looks for early evidence of hyperactivity, poor impulse control, brief attention span, low frustration threshold, and so on. It is always borne in mind that many people with ADD are members of the non-hyperactive sub-group. In such cases there is usually only a history of learning difficulties, lack of success in school and perhaps some problems with peer relationships.

Detailed history-taking eliminates other disorders or illnesses (such as seizure disorders, generalised systematic illnesses, personality disorders) and social and environmental factors that can also cause the symptoms mentioned in the previous paragraph. History-taking is therefore important because the similar symptoms these illnesses produce could contribute to a misleading clinical profile suggesting ADD.

After taking a careful history, the physician has a fair idea whether someone has ADD or not. To confirm a suspicion of ADD and to determine the extent of the problem, two further, specialised investigations may be performed.

2. A psychological assessment can be made of the patient's cognitive abilities in verbal and non-verbal reasoning. Such a pyscho-educational assessment shows how the person acquires, processes and integrates information, and how well he recalls the execution of certain tasks. In this way a profile of relative cognitive strengths and weaknesses is compiled.

The psychological assessments of people with ADD reveal symptoms that are fairly characteristic of the condition. These people generally have quite a marked discrepancy between their verbal and non-verbal reasoning skills. (IQ tests reveal stronger verbal skills.) They often have a diminished ability to focus and sustain attention, as well as a weak short-term memory. This applies especially to their auditory abilities, and a minority also have difficulties with their visual processing and retentive skills.

Investigating these people's methods of approach to problems and their actual behaviour in dealing with them reveals factors such as impulsiveness, poor organisational skills, and lack of self-confidence. A personality profile gives further insight into many of the other emotional and behavioural features of ADD, such as anxiety and aggression.

There are several well-researched psychological strategies that can be used to coax out the persona of the adult with suspected ADD. These strategies involve evaluations of potential anxiety, depression, mood swings, excessive euphoria, and drug or alcohol dependency. It is also important to establish whether other serious psychiatric conditions that mimic ADD (such as schizophrenia or psycopathy) are present. (These are in addition to detailed history-taking, outlined on pages 79 to 80.)

The Wechsler Adult Intelligence Scale (Revised, WAIS-R, Wechsler, 1981) is one such psychological test that gives valuable insight into people's cognitive skills.

3. Neurophysiological measurement is an area of investigation that examines the neurophysiological status of the central nervous system. As previously mentioned, the main problem in ADD is an inappropriate transmission of messages between cells in various parts of the central nervous system. Computerised neurophysiological techniques, such as Neurometrics or BEAM, allow us to look at the way the nerve cells in a particular individual transmit impulses and relay messages.

These techniques provide a picture of the person's ability to process information in the different cognitive regions of the brain. Evaluations of the visual, auditory and other sensory processing centres, as well as of the motor-frontal cortex (where movement comes from), are translated into a computerised picture which gives an indirect view of the state of the central nervous system.

These techniques measure the speed and amplitude (power)

with which neuronal charges are transmitted between different regions of the brain. These measurements are then compared with the norm for that person's age to determine the variation from the average. A 'brain map' which indicates the deviation from normal brain activity is produced, allowing the physician to detect at a glance abnormalities in neural transmission. This procedure is referred to as quantitative electroencephalography, and Figure 3 (page 83) shows brain maps in a young adult with ADD before and after drug treatment. Here the deviation from the average occurs in the frontal lobe where the shading indicates an excessive slowing of neural transmission compared with the norm for that age. The patient's response to drug therapy is indicated in the second diagram, where shading indicates improved transmission which is more appropriate for the age.

The investigation may be further enhanced by making impulses occur in the brain artificially with stimulators which produce electrical charges (known as 'evoked potentials') such as a stroboscope (for visual stimuli) or earphones producing click sounds (for auditory stimuli).

These artificially produced charges are measured as they travel between nerve cells, and their speed and amplitude compared with normal values. By using these measurements physicians can develop brain maps of the neural transmission, and the pictures in Figure 4 (page 85) show an evoked potential in an adult with ADD before and after drug therapy. The before-therapy picture shows an asymmetry (the response gained in the right hemisphere is better than in the left), and fairly weak amplitude. After drug therapy the response is more centralised and the amplitude is greater in the left hemisphere.

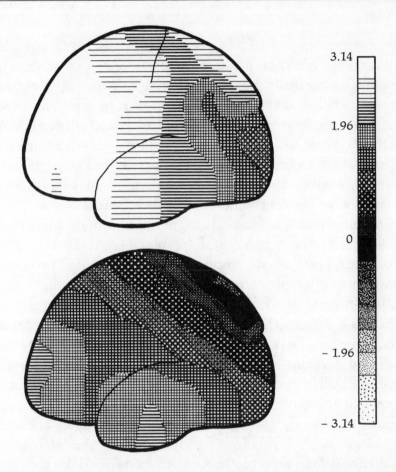

***Figure** 3 The results of a quantitative electroencephalogram (EEG) of a young adult, indicating the level of neural activity in his brain. The diagram on top illustrates the theta wave (slow wave) activity before drug therapy, the one below, after. The level of deviation from the norm for that age is indicated in the various shadings, each representing a different level of deviation as indicated on the scale. Very positive values, such as those obtained for the front area of the brain in the top diagram, indicate immaturity of these regions. The other diagram reveals that treatment with methylphenidate has decreased the patient's theta activity to a level more appropriate for his age, although not yet quite normal. This neurophysiological change was paralleled by an improvement in clinical test results.*

Neurometrics and BEAM are extremely useful in not only determining whether a person's central nervous system is functioning normally, but also whether it represents a certain category of behavioural or learning dysfunction. The brain maps they produce can be categorised as characteristic of ADD (with or without a learning disability), or schizophrenia, depression, dementia, and so on. Computerised electroneurophysiology gives the physician a much more sophisticated impression of the central nervous system function.

Computerised radiological techniques, where glucose is injected into the patient and its metabolism in the brain is photographed by a computerised scanner (PET, positron emission tomography), have also been utilised in adults with ADD. The rate at which the brain cells consume the glucose produces a pattern that can be related to normal or abnormal functioning. These techniques have so far consistently produced patterns indicating abnormal functioning in people with ADD. However, the expense of such investigations is great and they are not widely used at the time of writing.

Both psychology and neurophysiology techniques are used for diagnosing ADD and for monitoring the effects of treatment. When a person is being treated for ADD, the tests may be repeated after a period, and usually an improvement in the various cognitive skills shows up in the Wechsler test or the neurophysiology test. The tests are therefore extremely useful for determining whether the management programme for that particular person has been successful or not.

With the employment of these assessment methods — clinical, psychological and neurophysiological — the physician is in a good position to confirm whether ADD is present, and to estimate its extent and severity. He or she can also monitor

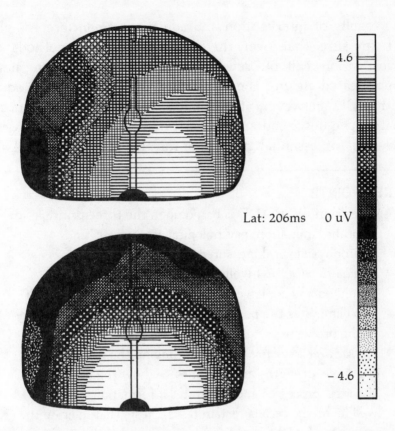

Lat: 206ms   0 uV

4.6

– 4.6

Figure 4 *Neurometrics evoked potential studies produce brain maps of the impulses travelling between neurons in the brain. This figure shows brain maps obtained from tests on the visual cognitive ability of a patient, and therefore tests cognitive functioning of the visual cortex (occipital lobe). The scale indicates the power of the impulse registered in the visual cortex. High power is indicated by positive values, low power by negative ones. The first brain map of this young man shows power that is weak and asymmetrically located, with maximum registration occurring in the right hemisphere. After medication there is an improvement in the evoked potentials, represented by the increased power and centralisation of the response, with almost as much of the impulse being received in the left hemisphere as in the right. Again, the patient also improved in clinical tests.*

the results of intervention and adjust treatment accordingly.

I am sure that over the next decade new methods of investigation will be developed to give us an even more sophisticated view of the central nervous system of the adult with ADD. However, at this stage the methods of diagnosis that I have described are reliable and reproducible, and form the basis of essential treatment for the person with ADD.

KEY POINTS

- The diagnosis of ADD is based upon the three principles of clinical examination, psychological assessment, and neurophysiological measurement.
  Clinical examination: Involves examining the patient's childhood and adolescent history for evidence of ADD. It also eliminates the possibility of other disorders and causes of the problems.
- *Psychological assessment:* Involves studying the patient's cognitive strengths and weaknesses (how the person acquires, processes and integrates information, and how well he or she recalls certain tasks). Tests that indicate the presence of ADD reveal much better verbal than non-verbal reasoning skills, a diminished ability to focus and sustain attention, a weak short-term memory, impulsiveness, et cetera.
- *Neurophysiological measurement:* As mentioned, the main problem in ADD is the inappropriate transmission of messages in the central nervous system. Computerised neurophysiological techniques allow doctors to study this. 'Brain maps' indicate the deviation from normal brain

KEY POINTS (continued)

activity, allowing the physician to detect abnormalities in neural transmission. They also indicate whether the results are due to ADD or some other problem. The maps also reveal improved brain activity after drug therapy.

CHAPTER FOURTEEN

DRUG THERAPY

The search for the magic bullet is something that is common to all disciplines in medicine. It would be true to say that most physicians seek a cure or remedy that is free of side-effects for the condition they are treating. Such has been the impetus for the development of many drugs, including: antibiotics (once penicillin was discovered by Fleming and Florey); the vaccine against polio, by Sabin and Salk (which had a crucial effect upon the lives of many young people in preventing its crippling paralysis); and beta-adrenergic stimulants, such as Ventolin (which have brought great relief to most asthma sufferers and even prevented death in many instances).

The search for a magic bullet for ADD has been going on for the last sixty years. Today several medications successfully treat ADD with very few side-effects. As with antibiotics, where no single antibiotic cures all illnesses, and with the polio vaccine, where different vaccines had to be developed for the three different strains of polio, so do we have different medications that work at different synoptic sites of the neo-cortex, the area affected by ADD.

Medication in ADD functions very much like the conductor of an orchestra. An orchestra has different groups of instruments such as strings, woodwinds, brass, percussion, and so on. Each group practises its own particular part of the music, but it is necessary for the conductor to bring them all together so that the resulting sound is harmonious and pleasing. Similarly, in ADD the various methods of treatment — behavioural control; remedial education for learning difficulties; specialised intervention for co-ordination or speech problems; and psychological intervention for personality disorders — are all essential in their own way to the overall improvement of the condition. However, it is often the case that only when medication is introduced to improve the neural transmission in the central nervous system do all these various strategies pull together and a co-ordinated result is obtained.

In Chapter 3 I discussed the neurobiological basis for ADD and indicated what mechanisms are involved. Remember that the main difficulty is the diminished transmission of the neurotransmitters, noradrenaline and dopamine, from one cell to the next. This is due to one or more of several factors, such as deficient production of the neurotransmitters themselves, their excessive destruction by enzymes, reabsorption of the neurotransmitters into the releasing cell, or poor binding with the receptor sites on the membrane of the succeeding cell.

The activity of the drugs that work in ADD takes place at these various sites. Certainly, we know that these medications improve the production and release of neurotransmitters into the synaptic cleft (the area between the brain cells), impede their destruction by the enzymes, and prevent their reabsorption into the preceding cell. Clear-cut evidence of improved binding with the receptor sites on the succeeding cell is not yet available. However, the evidence suggests that some of the medications that we use produce this effect.

PSYCHOSTIMULANTS

The psychostimulants were the first medications found to be useful in the treatment of ADD. In 1937 it was discovered that dexamphetamine had a significant benefit — it

improved the behaviour and learning of a group of children who had the characteristics of ADD. From that time
on, dexamphetamine was used in the treatment of such
children and was the subject of intense research. Later, a
second medication — methylphenidate — was also released;
it seemed to have properties similar to those of dexamphetamine. The chemical structure of the psychostimulants is
very similar to that of the neurotransmitters dopamine
and noradrenaline. It seems therefore, that their successful action is largely due to their similarity to
neurotransmitters.

The psychostimulants appear to work because of their
ability to increase the production of neurotransmitters and
to block the enzymatic destruction and re-uptake into the
releasing cell. There is little doubt that the psychostimulants
are the most successful medications for this condition. They
treat somewhere between 50 and 70 per cent of all people
with ADD. They are short-acting and have a clinical effect
in children of approximately 4 hours; in adults, they may be
effective for up to 6 hours.

When the diagnosis is correct, and the person's response
to this medication properly assessed and found to be
appropriate, no significant side-effects usually emerge. When
they do, the most common are those of some appetite loss
as well as mild insomnia. There are other, minor side-effects
that can be avoided by adjusting the dose.

Studies of adults with ADD indicate that the success rate
of treatment with these medications is very similar to that
for children with ADD. They therefore remain the drugs of
first choice in treating this condition in adults.

OTHER MEDICATIONS

As mentioned in the previous paragraph, most people with ADD respond well to the psychostimulants. However, there are significant numbers who do not respond to the psychostimulants and, in fact, may have adverse reactions to these drugs (such as loss of appetite, insomnia, tics or marked behavioural changes). It is therefore of great comfort to know that there are alternative medications available. These medications are as follows:

1. Moclobemide

Moclobemide is an inhibitor of the enzymes that destroy neurotransmitters in the synaptic cleft. Its action is of short duration (approximately 4 hours) and is reversible. This drug is therefore very useful where the enzymatic destruction of neurotransmitters is the main inhibitory factor. Moclobemide appears to have very few, if any, side-effects. It can be taken in relatively small doses for successful results. It was initially released on the market as a major antidepressant, but it also seems to benefit people with ADD.

2. Clonidine

Clonidine has been used for many years and with great success as an anti-hypertensive. It is not quite clear what its mode of action is, but it may be involved in inhibiting noradrenaline production or in the binding with the receptor sites. Its mode of action is longer than that of the psychostimulants, lasting approximately 12 hours. The side-effects associated with this medication are most commonly some initial drowsiness or irritability. Its major effect apparently concerns the behavioural features of ADD, improving the impulsiveness, frustration, mood swings and inflexibility.

3. Tricyclic Antidepressants

The most common successful tricyclic for treating ADD is imipramine. Here again the precise mode of action is not quite clear, but it is accepted that imipramine's function is to block the re-uptake of neurotransmitters into the releasing cell. Its duration of action is also approximately 4 to 6 hours. The most common side-effects are irritability, fatigue or some gastric disturbance. Other antidepressants include Bupropion which has a longer half life of 14 hours.

4. Thioridazine

Thioridazine is often used for younger children with ADD and certainly benefits both learning and behavioural difficulties. It also appears to help some adults with this condition and certainly should be considered where other treatments are not appropriate. Its mode of action is also unclear but probably concerns the receptor sites of the succeeding cell. Its major side-effects are weight gain, drowsiness and sleep disorder.

The treatment of ADD is an area of active research, not only for physicians but also for drug companies. I am quite sure that in a few years we will have a wider selection of medications that are more specific for the different mechanisms involved in ADD.

I would like to emphasise again that drug treatment in ADD is a crucial feature in the management of this condition. However, it should always be used in conjunction with the other strategies that have been set out in this book. Combining these other interventions with drug therapy means that not only are the features of ADD coped with but in many instances they become positive influences in people's lives.

KEY POINTS

- Several drugs successfully treat ADD, and have very few side-effects.
- Different medications work on different neurological sites of the brain.
- Medication in ADD works as the conductor of an orchestra: behavioural control, remedial education for learning difficulties, specialised intervention for co-ordination or speech problems, et cetera, often only pull together to achieve a result when medication to improve neural transmission is employed.
- Psychostimulants are the most successful medications for ADD. They appear to work because of their similarity to the neurotransmitters; they increase production of the neurotransmitters, block their enzymatic destruction and re-uptake into the releasing cell. They produce no significant side-effects, except for occasionally causing mild loss of appetite or insomnia.
- For those who do not respond to the psychostimulants and have adverse reactions to them, alternative medications are available.
- Drug treatment in ADD is a crucial feature in the management of this condition, which should always be used in conjunction with the other strategies outlined in this book.

CHAPTER FIFTEEN

PROGNOSIS

It seems to me that the biological rhythm of life is probably determined at conception, or even perhaps before then. Each healthy person's life has a unique pulse or measure that inexorably carries us from birth to death and, apart from living sensibly, eating well and attending to our health, there is not much else that we can do, physically, to influence it. However, with the proper development and care of our *mental* health, we can, to a certain extent, influence our biological rhythm, and in this way improve the quality of our lives.

As we have seen in previous chapters, there is a natural tendency in an organism towards a state of balance between what appear to be opposite or contrasting elements: in the nervous system there is a balance between the secretion of neurotransmitters and their destruction by enzymes; there is also a balance between the stimulation from the diencephalon and inhibition from the higher-seated neocortex. This balance exists at a higher plane as well, and the entire human organism depends on a system of equilibrium between two opposites: such as the physical and the emotional; the physical and the intellectual; and the carnal and the spiritual. The essence of the unconscious balancing that we engage in our daily lives is to bring harmony to these opposing influences and in this way to ensure that we maintain an overall state of well-being.

ADD is a condition that disturbs and disrupts this internal balance, so that the biophysical side of the equation assumes a greater importance and reduces the state of mental health on the other side of the equation. The physical results — hyperactivity, impulsiveness, diminished co-ordination and speech abilities — skew the equilibrium on the physical side, while the reduction in concentration, memory and self-esteem, along with the high levels of anger, frustration and inflexibility undermine the mental side of the equation, further upsetting the final balance. The wholistic management of ADD is therefore directed at resorting this balance and returning to people with the condition some influence over the natural rhythm of their lives.

In preceding chapters I discussed the various means of coping with the dysfunctions caused by ADD that affect both physical and mental health. I outlined how the appropriate management of ADD helps to reduce its adverse effects, accentuate its positive features, and restore balance. These measures include efforts exerted by the individuals themselves, such as in channelling excess energy or containing impulsiveness, as well as more passive assistance such as drug therapy. Balance is achieved only when all such factors have been comprehensively attended to.

Learning more about your ADD through becoming aware of the various problems it can cause will benefit you immensely. Once you know how ADD affects those who have it and which symptoms you personally possess, you will be better able to understand your behaviour. Keep an eye on your responses, and watch out for those that are affected by your ADD.

Changing patterns of behaviour, often ones that we have followed all our lives, takes lots of time and effort. Be patient with yourself. Don't be discouraged if you think that all your attempts to correct a certain behaviour aren't working, or you notice yourself repeating a behaviour that you thought you had under control — with perseverance you will gradually learn to manage your ADD.

Only through awareness and understanding will you begin to take charge of your ADD rather than it taking charge of you. In fact, as stated earlier in this book, many people with ADD develop — either consciously or unconsciously — their own methods of overcoming the problems this condition brings. If this describes you, well done! However, you will still find that learning more about your ADD will only benefit you.

Talking with those close to you about the way this condition affects you and how you attempt to control it will also prove worthwhile. Family, friends and close workmates can let you know when your efforts are producing results — results that not only benefit you but that are also appreciated by others.

Most importantly, seek professional help so that you can be fully assessed, correctly diagnosed and have a management plan worked out for you. This could include psychological, behavioural, social and relationship strategies, as well as possible medication.

RETIREMENT
One matter I have not mentioned so far in this book is planning for retirement. It is hoped that by the time a person with ADD reaches retirement they can look forward to relaxation and contentment. This will be the case when proper provision has been made for retirement.

Retirement is as much an active process as all other stages of our lives. It should be anticipated and planned for much the same as our daily activities are, with the main difference being that at retirement the driving forces that make us regularly employ our physical and mental energies come to an abrupt halt. Unless this change in our lives is planned for, it could once again disrupt and disorganise our balance.

I suggest, therefore, that during the active periods of your life you take time and effort to develop interests and activities that you can pursue after retirement and that would continue to enhance your life as well as your value to other people.

In other words, pursue interests, hobbies and recreational activities not only for their benefits in your active years but also retirement. It is a well-known fact that people with ADD tend to be somewhat inflexible in their thinking and focus on what is necessary for the moment. In this way the pursuit of career opportunities and success in the workplace is often considered sufficient in itself to these people and they do not allow themselves time or space to pursue other interests. It is therefore imperative to cultivate activities and pastimes that can replace the work ethic when retirement commences.

Overactive people could take up sports to keep them physically occupied and to help channel their energies successfully. People who are intellectually overactive could develop hobbies, such as chess or bridge or even travel, to satisfy their cerebral energy. Consider joining clubs or committees for social intercourse and to prevent isolation from the community. Married people should plan activities in close consultation with their partners, because the balance between the two of them is just as crucial as their individual internal balance. Single people should consider those who are closest to them and work out how they are able to enrich these relationships.

There is no doubt in my mind that by properly employing the principles I have highlighted here, you will be in a better position to improve the quality of your working life and retirement. Keep in mind that no single activity or stage in your life exists in isolation, and that each process is related to the previous one, and give full attention to your mental and spiritual needs as much as to your physical requirements. If we do all this, we are in a better situation to contribute to those around us, and they in turn will reflect our contribution in their attitude and behaviour toward us. This balance between us and our immediate surroundings is crucial to our ultimate contentment.

KEY POINTS

- As outlined in this book, there are means of coping with the dysfunctions caused by ADD. The appropriate management of the disorder reduces its adverse effects, and can even turn the disadvantages it brings to advantages.
- Learning more about your ADD will help you to control it.
- Be patient with yourself when trying to change established patterns of behaviour.
- Talking with family and close friends can help you monitor your behaviour, and let you know when your efforts to change it are producing results.
- Most importantly, seek professional help.
- During your younger, more active years, take time to develop interests that you can pursue after your retirement.
- Managing your ADD and paying attention to and balancing all aspects of your life — your work, social, mental, physical and spiritual needs — are crucial to your ultimate happiness.

CHAPTER SIXTEEN

LESSONS FROM HISTORY

It is with great truth that the prophet writing the Book of Ecclesiastes in the Old Testament states that 'nothing is new under the sun'. What is happening today very likely happened in the past and in all probability will happen again in the future. However, we are often limited by our failure to take advantage of the lessons provided us by events of the past. I have always felt that if we are aware of what has gone before us, we can often gain profitably from other people's experiences. It is for this reason that I would like to share with you the experiences of four great men who undoubtedly had ADD throughout their lives. I will briefly sketch their individual characteristics and then show what they did that made them successful and able to overcome the disadvantages of ADD.

WINSTON CHURCHILL

Winston Churchill had everything going for him from birth. He was born into the aristocracy, being the grandson of the seventh Duke of Marlborough. He was descended from the distinguished and famous families of the first Earl of Spencer and John Churchill, the first Duke of Marlborough, who had been one of the most successful soldiers in the history of Europe. His mother was American. She came from one of the blue-blooded families on the eastern seaboard who counted amongst their ancestors soldiers who had fought for General Washington during the American War of Independence.

However, ADD was a condition that seemed to be pervasive throughout the family. When you read the life of John Churchill, the first Duke of Marlborough, you realise that he was a very active person, often impetuous but with a very generous and expansive personality. Winston Churchill's father, Lord Randolph Churchill, showed distinct features of ADD that included an excessive activity level and poor ability to concentrate — evident in his rambling speeches in Parliament. His other symptoms — low frustration threshold and extreme heights of anger — often intimidated and estranged the young Winston. Randolph Churchill was also quite impulsive and this was most notably evident when he impetuously tendered his resignation from the ministry, thinking that it would be refused and that he would perhaps be offered a more senior position. Unfortunately, his resignation was accepted and he never saw the Cabinet room again.

As a young boy Winston was certainly very active and lively. He himself later stated that he was 'what grown-up people in their offhand way call a troublesome boy'. He was always into mischief. After the birth of his younger brother, his mother complained to his father that Winston never stopped teasing the baby and she was going to 'take him in hand'. When he went to school Winston had great difficulty in paying attention and was often accused of being a day-dreamer. He never completed work in the classroom and his homework was seldom done. He seemed to have a poor short-term memory, especially at the auditory level, and had problems retaining verbal information. He was usually late for classes. He was disorganised and had poor fine-motor control, as evident by his slow handwriting. However, he had excellent gross-motor co-ordination and excelled at certain sports, including fencing. His success at fencing was due not only to his good co-ordination but also to his daring and impulsiveness, by which he frequently surprised his opponents by the rapid thrust of his attack.

As a young man Winston often proved to be obstinate and inflexible, particularly with people close to him, such as his parents and teachers. His obstinacy was often seen as arrogance and even his mother once accused him of this. However, nothing could deter Winston from being forceful when he felt the need to press a certain argument.

His poor short-term recall certainly affected his scholastic progress. He once failed a Latin examination at Harrow because he could not remember one single word of the particular translation. Later he complained that he had never translated Latin into English, but his tutor asserted that she had been translating Virgil and Caesar with him for more than a year. These memory blanks affected him on several occasions in his life. However, he had excellent *visual* short-term memory and later in life could recall in great detail his experiences in South Africa during the Boer War, in India and the Middle East.

Churchill performed with mediocrity at school. He did better at linguistic subjects such as English and history, but was quite dreadful at mathematics. He admitted to a great deal of laziness and found himself indolent for prolonged periods, which caused him great pain and stress, and which he worked to overcome throughout his life. Like most people with ADD, he did not lack diligence or energy when he was pursuing something in which he had a great interest. (Characteristically of people with ADD, this interest level is often of a narrow focus, and anything that falls outside it receives much less application. Overcoming this narrow focus is one of the challenges that faces such people.)

When Churchill left school he was enrolled in Sandhurst Military College and pursued a career in the Army. This was a useful venture as it gave sufficient scope for his excessive energy and impulsiveness, and eventually gave him the opportunity to travel the world — sometimes as a soldier and sometimes as a war correspondent. He was often involved in battles in which he came close to death. However, he always stayed cool and calm in the middle of conflict and was fortunate enough to escape unharmed. One wonders whether this calm, collected attitude was due more to his impulsiveness and lack of perception than to his undoubted bravery. I am sure that there was a mixture of both in Winston Churchill.

During his younger years he discovered his interest and exceptional flair for speech-making and writing. He developed these talents after he left the Army, and became a politician, war correspondent and novelist. Churchill possessed an uncanny ability to grasp immediately situations that were complex and apparently insoluble, and then render these complexities into simple terms so that they could be understood by the general public. It was for this reason that his essays and writings on the situations in South Africa, Cuba, the Middle East and Spain were so well received. These gifts also served him admirably in later years when he became the war-time Prime Minister that led Great Britain to its victory over the Germans.

Without question, Churchill's ability to seize the essence of a problem and simplify it into its components is what brought him so quickly to the solution of a particular conflict. He also had the forcefulness (or impulsiveness) to pursue any solution with great zeal. Sometimes these pursuits resulted in disaster, such as in some of the battles and strategy decisions of the Second World War, but more often they were dramatically successful.

However, Churchill was always at risk of becoming too involved in his pursuits, and at times he had to be reminded of this by his wife, Clementine. She was a very necessary antidote to his frequent excesses and, like his nanny in childhood, Mrs Everest, was able often to bring him to a point of clearer thinking.

Mention must be made of the order and discipline imposed on Churchill as a boy and young man in the schools he attended. I doubt that he would have achieved as well in life, and certainly not as early as he did, if he had not been placed in institutions that provided him with the principles of structure and order that remained with him for the rest of his life. Despite his ambivalence about his schooldays, there is no doubt that they stood him in good stead in later life.

LUDWIG van BEETHOVEN

Beethoven was also born to a family with a history of hyperactivity and ADD. His grandfather, certainly one of the early teachers of the young Beethoven, was a musician at the court of the Elector Archbishop of Bonn and that is where Beethoven's father grew up and where Beethoven himself was born. He was not born to a wealthy family; his father was also a musician and sang tenor in the choir at the court of the Elector, and his mother was a chambermaid and the daughter of a cook.

Beethoven's father was a man of very bad temper and was often referred to as unbalanced. He was impulsive and inconsistent and also seemed to be extremely active, if not over-active. He was generally inflexible in his attitude towards his family and to his children in particular. He was given to alcoholism which affected his life in the long run. However, he was perceptive enough to realise that his son, Ludwig, was someone with enormous talents. Beethoven's mother, on the other hand, had a very sweet disposition and tried to shield her three sons from the frequent anger and intolerance of their father. She taught her children how to develop patience in the face of adversity, and compassion.

As a boy and young man Beethoven was described as shy but honest. He was resolute — perhaps obstinate — and often quite sad; he needed love, and sought it throughout his whole life.

Beethoven had difficulties with learning, and mathematics proved far too hard for him. He had great problems with his fine-motor control, which affected his handwriting skills and his musical abilities. Although he became an excellent pianist, he never quite mastered the technique of violin-playing because of the different sort of co-ordination it requires.

Beethoven's abilities as a musician and pianist became rapidly established in the court of Bonn, and eventually he went to Vienna where he met Haydn and Mozart. Both these composers remarked upon the great potential of the young boy from the provinces. Whilst in Vienna he displayed his pianistic skills in competition with other musicians and was always declared the victor. At all times he was convinced that his musical talent was exceptional. At one stage later in his life he complained about his disorganisation and inability to perform certain ordinary daily activities, but consoled himself that 'at least Beethoven knows how to write music'.

Although Beethoven was an extremely generous person, often impulsively so, he was also considered rude and insensitive to others' feelings. He tended to offend others with his impulsiveness, only to regret it just as quickly. He also had excessive energy and felt the need to go on regular long walks every day, no doubt to help dissipate some of it. He encountered problems in organising his life and certainly had lifelong difficulties with handling money. He seemed to be impulsive in this area as well. However, he did set himself a rigorous daily routine which consisted of some work in the morning upon rising, followed by a long cold shower, and then coffee afterwards — an exercise characterised by his habit of counting out exactly sixty grains of coffee. This was another indication of his obsessiveness, a frequent feature of ADD. After that he went for a walk and visited antique shops. In the afternoon he spent a lengthy period working, followed by another walk, before retiring in the evening.

Beethoven was a person who felt passions and emotions almost at an above-human level. However, he was never able to establish a longstanding relationship with any particular woman. He had many love affairs but did not marry. This may reflect a certain amount of emotional ineptitude or even lack of self-esteem concerning women.

Despite his growing deafness, Beethoven became one of the greatest artistic geniuses of all time, but certainly not without significant cost to himself as an individual. Almost subconsciously, he must have sacrificed many elements of normal human existence such as love, companionship and sociability to attain his musical achievements. However, when one looks at the disadvantages with which he was born — especially his learning disabilities, fine-motor co-ordination difficulties and impulsiveness, the magnitude of his achievements can be better appreciated.

SAMUEL JOHNSON

Samuel Johnson was one of England's greatest men of letters. He was greatly admired by the intellects of his time for his independence of thought and for his talents for going to the heart of the matter and resolving it simply and lucidly. He was a person of great learning in many fields and his company was sought out by the famous and wealthy not only in England, but in Europe. Johnson, however, was born to a humble family in Staffordshire at the start of the eighteenth century. His father was a bookseller and bookbinder, although his mother came from a slightly more established family.

While at school Johnson displayed remarkable knowledge about topics of the day and ability to discuss them, and he seemed to have an excellent long-term memory. He appeared to be quite precocious about contemporary issues and was not backward in putting his ideas forward. Throughout schooling the teachers remarked upon his independence of spirit which of course led to clashes with authority.

It is from these early years that Samuel Johnson displayed the features of ADD which affected him throughout his life and kept him struggling against them. He was prone to extreme bursts of activity which verged on hyperactivity and he often did things too hastily, which occasionally led to disasters. He was also impatient, impulsive, and to a certain extent intolerant.

These episodes of hyperactivity were counterbalanced by others of severe indolence, during which he achieved nothing, and throughout his life Samuel Johnson struggled against them. Even when he was an old and established man of letters, he experienced these severe episodes of indolence and not even the best entreaties from his friends could then encourage him to be productive.

Like many people with ADD he was a severe procrastinator. He would have enormously brilliant ideas and would like to have executed them, but always seemed to be putting off until tomorrow what he could have done that particular day. This was especially noticeable when he went to Oxford for one year; he was full of promise but many people complained that he seemed to waste his time and did not study hard enough.

Samuel Johnson had great difficulties with concentration when it came to reading. His difficulty was not in understanding a text but in actually reading it through completely and thoroughly. He tended to skim books, grasping the content from just a few sentences, and he was notorious for seldom finishing the books he began. An inability to finish things in general, but especially reading, is a common feature of ADD.

Samuel Johnson intuitively felt that his indolence and disorganised daily routine would spoil his success as an intellectual, and so from early days he worked at his laziness by forcing himself to rise early in the morning and impose a certain order on his daily life. It was only when these daily routines were successful that he was most productive in his literary pursuits.

Johnson also displayed one of the features of ADD more commonly seen in the younger person: tics or habit spasms (involuntary motor movements). These are common in people with ADD and are characterised by uncontrolled head movements, eye-blinking, lip-twitching, throat-clearing or other noise-making, and some are even more elaborate than these. Throughout his life Johnson had tics that caused him much embarrassment.

Social imperception sometimes spoiled his interaction with others. Many accounts have described him as having been very rude to friends or to tutors, without perhaps fully realising it.

Despite all these ADD limitations, Johnson worked assiduously at overcoming them and with notable results. When he found that things were getting too much for him, he used arithmetic to steady his mind and impose some self-discipline. He would then break things up into manageable units to give him perspective on a certain problem, write them down and solve them individually before tackling the whole problem again. He was eventually able to contain his impulsive, impetuous nature and his indolence, and to improve his self-esteem. The end result was a person who is still regarded as one of the greatest people of England.

ALBERT EINSTEIN

Albert Einstein is the architect of modern science and physics. His theories on relativity, gravitation and quantum mechanics are still vital to our modern scientific endeavours. He is in effect the father of the atomic bomb, although he himself was totally opposed to its development and use. However, he is the successor to that other great scientist, Sir Isaac Newton, whom Einstein admired for his great originality and dedication of purpose.

Einstein was born to a fairly humble German-Jewish family that was not religiously orthodox. Perhaps because of his unconventional upbringing, Einstein at the age of twelve years came to the conclusion that there was no such thing as a personal God. This, he felt, gave him enormous freedom to pursue his ideas.

As a young boy Einstein had significant learning problems. First, as he was very late with his speech development and did not form two-word sentences before the age of four or five. It was thought for some time that he was perhaps mentally retarded.

He also had tremendous difficulties with his concentration and was a notorious day-dreamer. In class he was always thinking about things other than the lesson given at the time, which alarmed his teachers and parents. Einstein had difficulties in learning his lessons, including his reading and writing. The only things that he could concentrate on were arithmetic and science.

Eventually when he left school, he did not have any qualifications for proper employment. He joined his parents in Milan and renounced his German citizenship. He was to remain stateless for many years until he settled in the United States of America.

Unlike most dropouts he did continue to study privately, especially mathematics. Eventually his father's business in Switzerland failed and Albert had to support himself by working. Since it was thought that he would perhaps do well in electrical engineering, he enrolled at the Swiss Federal Polytechnics School, but failed the general entrance examination. However, he had performed extremely well in the mathematical section of the exam and the director of the

Polytechnics School suggested that he work for a diploma at the Swiss High School and then reapply. This Einstein did and he was accepted without further examination.

In mathematics Einstein's ability to break problems down into their components and thereby solve them stood him in great stead. He wrote: 'In this field, however, I soon learnt to scent out that which was able to lead to fundamentals and to turn aside from everything else, from the multitude of things which clutter up the mind and divert it from the essential'. Einstein was able to realise that to reach the core of a problem he had to strip it of the clutter in the way of the fundamentals.

It is clear, then, that as a young man Albert Einstein had difficulty with concentration. He was a restless individual who often found it difficult to settle, he had problems imposing order and discipline upon his daily life, and he had significant problems with his auditory perception, and this had an adverse effect on his learning abilities (leading to linguistic difficulties rather than mathematical ones).

Personally, Einstein was a gentle person who related well to other people. Although he had two marriages, he was generally able to balance his scientific pursuits with domestic life. It seems, therefore, that his ADD was of a kind without hyperactivity or the other behavioural features that go with that particular ADD subgroup. When he brought the dysfunctions of his condition under control, he was then able to release his energies in his chosen field and become the most successful scientist of this century.

These are a few examples of men with ADD who have achieved much, in spite of, and sometimes because of, their difficulties. The four described above have a few characteristics in common that seem to have made them all equally successful. First, each one found what he was good at and what would also keep him interested enough to satisfy his energies: Churchill with his oration, Beethoven with his composition, Johnson with his world of literature and Einstein with his pursuit of science and mathematics. Once they had determined which of their talents set them above others, they pursued that skill with admirable relentlessness. It is this tenacity in developing their talents that ultimately made them successful.

A third element of their success is their effort to set a rigorous routine in their daily lives. By setting themselves a firm structure of rising in the morning, bathing, eating, working, resting and walking, they were able to free their minds for more demanding pursuits.

Certainly, they all had serious limitations and shortcomings. But they refused to allow these to dominate their lives, and achieved success by the sheer mental imposition of their will upon the physical aspects of their existences. In this way they overcame the negative aspects of ADD while at the same time they made the most of its positive features, with notable success.

DR GORDON SERFONTEIN

Paediatric Neurologist, author, father and family man.

Gordon Serfontein was born in 1942 in South Africa. He trained as a children's neurologist in North America, where he became interested in the modern methods used to manage children with Specific Learning Disabilities (SLD) and Attention Deficit Disorder (ADD).

Gordon realised that he had suffered from ADD as a child and knew firsthand how it felt. For him school had been a shambles, but by his teenage years his intellect had broken through and after that nothing could stop him. He entered the Air Force as a trainee pilot and became dux of his year. As a man used to flying jets at high speed, once he entered medicine he was not going to allow unenlightened professionals to block his path.

In 1980 when Gordon arrived in Australia, most child psychiatrists believed ADD was a problem of parenting and poor environment. Gordon came into conflict with this view because he believed children with ADD were born with a minor difference in their brains and, although environmental factors could make their symptoms worse, the primary condition was not the fault of the parents. Gordon removed the guilt from parents, helped them to restructure the child's environment and treated the difference in the brain with stimulant medication. Many professionals claimed his methods were dangerous and unproven. Some psychiatrists believed that he colluded with parents, stopping them from facing up to their own responsibilities in causing their child's problems.

In the early 1980s, Gordon found working in Sydney extremely uncomfortable. He considered leaving Australia but when he saw how disruptive this would be to his young family he decided to 'tough it out'. He set up a small private clinic staffed by his wife, Barbara, and one secretary. The demand for his help increased rapidly and by the end of the decade he had employed a large team of doctors, psychologists and remedial teachers. He had also been asked to set up similar services in Brisbane, Auckland and London.

Gordon worked extremely hard, but medicine was only one part of his life. He loved to be with his wife and their five children. He read widely, followed the arts and could speak several languages. In his youth he had been a keen sportsman and continued this interest from the sidelines at the rugby and cricket. Gordon had a great love of English cars, driving and tinkering with anything from Morris 1000s to Jaguars.

Gordon worked for many years before he got the recognition he deserved. Even in the late 1980s when he approached publishers with his book *The Hidden Handicap*, initially no one would touch it, such was the misinformation spread by those antagonistic to his views.

Now most of Gordon's ideas have been fully accepted and are used all over Australia. I don't believe that this change of attitude came about by Gordon influencing his detractors — it was brought about by the thousands of parents who had experienced his help. They knew he was right and forced the professionals to move with the times.

Early last year Gordon left to spend some time with his elderly mother in South Africa. He became unexpectedly ill on the flight and never made it back to his home in Australia.

When I delivered the eulogy at Gordon's memorial service, extra seats had to be put in the church, such were the number of parents moved to attend. One mother summed it up in a letter: 'I just had to write to you regarding the untimely death of a wonderful man. In fact I have been so shocked that it has taken me this long to compose myself enough to put my thoughts on paper.' She went on to talk of how her son had been helped for over nine years and the massive difference it had made to all their lives:

> My son is devastated by the loss of Gordon, he has always believed that only two people have ever understood him, his mother and of course Gordon. Gordon was always discredited by the teachers at my son's school, but I fought them all the way. Gordon not only helped hundreds of children, but indirectly saved marriages as well. I know he prevented me from having a nervous breakdown. I am, and always will be, deeply indebted to him for his fight to have ADD recognised and accepted. I know there is not much I can do, but if it is at all possible, can you please let his family know how much we all loved and respected him and how the entire community is the poorer for his passing. We have lost a wonderful, kind, courageous and clever man. He really cared.

In Australia, the recognition and treatment of children with ADD has undergone a revolution largely through the efforts of one man. Gordon's next crusade was to raise the awareness of adult ADD and to set up some services. Unfortunately he died before he completed his work. This book will increase the awareness, it will fall to those who follow to set up the services.

Dr Christopher Green
Sydney, March 1994

GLOSSARY

Central nervous system: that portion of the nervous system consisting of the brain and spinal cord by means of which sensations are co-ordinated and responses organised.

Cognitive skills: the skills involved in that activity of the mind by which we become aware of objects of thought or perception. It includes all aspects of perceiving, thinking and remembering.

Cerebral cortex: a thin layer of grey matter on the surface of the cerebral hemispheres consisting of neuronal brain cells.

Diencephalon (see also, limbic system): the central part of the forebrain (consisting of paired masses of nervous tissue surrounding the third ventricle).

Dopamine: a chemical that acts as a neurotransmitter.

Dysfunction: the disturbance, impairment or abnormality of the functioning of an organ.

Evoked potentials: the voltage occurring as the result of stimulation applied to a nerve.

Hyperactivity: a mental state where there is a high level of body movement, thought processes and talkativeness.

Inhibitory neuron: a neurone that inhibits the transmission of a stimulus.

Limbic system (see also, diencephalon): a functionally related set of neural structures in the region of the mid-brain, activated during emotional arousal and motivated behaviour.

Neocortex: all of the cerebral cortex, except the hippocampus and piriform areas. This area is responsible for the remarkable powers of reasoning and intelligence in humans.

Nerve: a bundle of nerve fibres along which impulses pass.

Neuron: any of the conducting cells of the nervous system.

Neurophysiological: the way in which the nervous system functions.

Neurotransmitters: substances allowing the passage of impulses along and between nerve cells.

Noradrenaline: a hormone with transmitter properties.

Occipital lobes: the most posterior part of the cerebrum.

Stimulatory neuron: neurons used to produce an electrical impulse to cause physiological stimulation.

Synapse: the microscopic area of proximity between two neurons.

Synaptic cleft: the space between the cell membranes of two neurons at a synapse.

BIBLIOGRAPHY

The quotes concerning Winston Churchill that are used at the beginning of many chapters in this book are taken from *Churchill: A Life* by Martin Gilbert (Octopus Publishing Group, a division of Reed International Books Limited, London, 1991).

The following indicates where quotes have been used in *ADD in Adults*, and then gives the page reference showing where they were taken from in *Churchill: A Life*. They are reproduced with permission of Curtis Brown Ltd, London, on behalf of the Estate of Sir Winston Churchill. Copyright the Estate of Sir Winston S. Churchill.

Introduction, p. 6; Chapter 1, pp. 5–6; Chapter 2, p. 69; Chapter 4, pp. 35–6; Chapter 5, p. 119; Chapter 6, pp. 4–5; Chapter 7, pp. 70 and 80; Chapter 8, p. 29; Chapter 9, pp. 20–1; Chapter 10, p. 82; Chapter 11, p. 25; Chapter 12, p. 56; Chapter 13, p. 34.

Bellak, L., Black, R.B. 'Attention deficit hyperactivity disorder in adults, *Clinical Therapeutics*, 1992; 14:138–47.

Gittelmann, R., Mannuzza, S., Shenker, R., Bonagura, N. 'Hyperactive boys almost grown up: Psychiatric status', *Archives of General Psychiatry* 1985; 42:937–47.

Mann, L.S., et al. 'Quantitative analysis of EEG in boys with attention deficit hyperactivity disorder: Controlled study with clinical implications'. *Pediatric Neurology*, 1992, 8:30–6.

Mauer, K. (ed.). *Topographic brain mapping of EEG and evoked potentials*, Springer-Verlag, 1989.

Roy, John E., et al. 'Neurometric and behavioural studies', in *Perspectives on Dyslexia, Vol. 1*, John Wiley & Sons, 1990.

Shekim, W.O., Asarnow, R.F., Hess, E., Zaucha, K., Wheeler, N. 'A clinical and demographic profile of a sample of adults with attention deficit hyperactivity disorder, residual state', *Comp. Psychiatry*, 1990; 31:416–25.

Wender, P.W., Reimherr, F.W., Wood, D.R. 'Attention deficit disorder (Minimal brain dysfunction) in adults: A replication study of diagnosis and drug treatment', *Archives of General Psychiatry*, 1981; 38:449–56.

Wood, D.R., Reimherr, F.W., Wender, P.W. et al. 'Diagnosis and treatment of minimal brain dysfunction in adults: A preliminary report', *Archives of General Psychiatry*, 1976; 33:1453–60.

Zametkin, A.J., et al. 'Cerebral glucose metabolism in adults with hyperactivity of childhood onset', *New England Journal of Medicine*, 1990; 323:1361–66.

INDEX